God Is for the Alcoholic

Revised and Expanded

God Is for the Alcoholic

Revised and Expanded

by
Jerry Dunn

with
Bernard Palmer

MOODY PRESS
CHICAGO

Library of Congress Cataloging-in-Publication Data

Dunn, Jerry.
    God is for the alcoholic.

    Bibliography: p.
        1. Alcoholics—Rehabilitation—United States.
2. Alcoholism—Religious aspects—Christianity.
4. Alcoholism—United States. I. Palmer, Bernard
Alvin, 1914-   . II. Title.
HV5279.D86   1986   261.8'32292   86-8464
ISBN 0-8024-3284-0 (pbk.)

13526223

5 6 7 Printing/LC/Year 91 90 89

Printed in the United States of America

To my dear wife, Greta,
who stood by and believed God,
trusting Him to set me free

Contents

CHAPTER   PAGE

Preface   11

Part 1: *Understanding the Problem*   13

1. The Complexity of Alcoholism   15
   - What causes alcoholism?
   - Two types of alcoholics
   - Who are America's alcoholics?
   - Definition and effects of intoxication

2. The Seven Steps to Alcoholism (Steps 1-4)   31
   - Social drinking
   - Dependent drinking
   - Prealcoholic phase
   - Problem drinking

3. The Seven Steps to Alcoholism (Steps 5-7)   45
   - The dropover point
   - Chronic alcoholism
   - Organic deterioration

4. Completing the Cycle   59
   - The desire never to take another drink
   - The pride of sobriety
   - The fear of drinking again
   - The conviction that it has been mastered
   - The final step

5. The Family of the Alcoholic—Hindrance and Help   71
   - The alienation of the family
   - The family can hinder recovery
   - The family needs help
   - The family can help recovery

6. What God Says   87
   - What does the Bible say?
   - Should the Christian abstain?

Part 2: *Ways Others Can Help the Alcoholic*   95

7. Tap the Resources of Prayer   97
   - Be sure you are a member of God's family
   - Stand on God's promise to answer
   - Make the right approach
   - Be willing to be God's supply line
   - Don't forget to ask
   - Expect an answer

8. Present the Gospel   111
   - God's way is basic
   - Where do we begin?
   - God's love changes lives
   - Counseling takes time
   - Christianity is a way of life
   - Christianity is a new life

9. Provide Fellowship   119
   - The need for fellowship
   - The source of fellowship
   - The Samaritan principle
   - Hindrances to fellowship
   - Help for fellowship

10. Rely on God's Help   129
    - Psalm 37—the therapy psalm
    - The church's role
    - Alcoholics Anonymous and Alcoholics Victorious

11. Plan to Be Long-Suffering   145
    - Steps of intervention
    - Lessons from the prodigal son
    - Lessons from the prodigal's father
    - Lessons from the prodigal's brother

12. Practice Firmness   159
    - Let the alcoholic stand on his own two feet
    - Make ground rules
    - Protect your interests
    - Mean what you say
    - Don't do for him what he should do for himself
    - Ask advice
    - Actions speak louder than words
    - Breaking community dependence

13. Helping the Teenager   173
  • Where do they learn it?
  • Why do they drink?
  • What can we do?

14. Groups That Take Action   179
  • How we can help
  • MADD
  • SMART
  • SADD

Part 3: *Five Ways the Alcoholic Can Help Himself*   187

15. Transfer Your Dependency to God   189
  • You can't do it yourself
  • How I found God's love
  • Make the transfer
  • Start a new life
  • Grow through the Word

16. Talk with God Daily   199
  • The Lord's Prayer—an outline for talking with God

17. Give Yourself   211
  • Give yourself to God
  • Give yourself to others—to receive help
  • Give yourself to others—to find fellowship
  • Give yourself to others—to provide help
  • Give your money

18. Live a Step at a Time   221
  • Physical considerations
  • Forming new habits
  • Renewing the mind
  • The Spirit-controlled life

19. Keep a Perpetual Inventory   231
  • Assets and Liabilities
  • Facing temptations

  Summary   237
  Suggested Reading   238
  Organizations for Alcoholics   239

Preface

I wrote *God Is for the Alcoholic* twenty years ago. More than 300,000 copies have now been sold. When it was first written my experience was limited to men at the Open Door Mission in Omaha, Nebraska, where I conducted the rehabilitation program for alcoholics. In 1969 my experience was expanded to include women and young people at our family ministry at the People's City Mission in Lincoln, Nebraska. That gave me insight into the terrible effects alcohol has on the families of alcoholics. Our goal was to help nondrinking family members transform their houses of chaos into homes of blessing.

During our stay in Lincoln I had the opportunity to serve on the board of the Lincoln Council on Alcoholism and Drugs. As chairman of their comprehensive planning committee, I had the privilege of helping to found the first detoxification center in the county and to help establish the Independent Center on Alcoholic Treatment in connection with Lincoln General Hospital.

As president of the International Union of Gospel Missions for the years 1971-1973 I was in contact with many alcoholic treatment programs throughout the United States where I saw the latest methods in the treatment of alcoholism being used. I also learned that the principles set down in *God Is for the Alcoholic* in 1965 are as valid today as they were twenty years ago. But treatment of alcoholism has not remained static. So newly developed methods have been incorporated into those already outlined in the book to make it even more effective. That is the reason for this revision.

I trust that you will be strengthened as you read the book and that as you apply its principles your alcoholic and the alcoholic family you are associated with might know the victory that is ours through Jesus Christ our Lord.

Part 1

Understanding the Problem

God is for the alcoholic! I discovered that for myself at the conclusion of a two-year drunk when I picked up a Bible in my Texas prison cell more than thirty-seven years ago. I have seen it proved over and over again in the lives of men and women in every stratum of society. There is hope for the alcoholic and his bewildered, suffering family. But alcoholism is such a confusing and complex problem that many of God's children do not know how to be used of Him in helping the alcoholic.

In these pages I hope to be able to give a little better understanding of the problem, the product, and the person of alcoholism. I hope to show how, under the direction of God, this helpless individual can be intelligently aided.

ONE
THE COMPLEXITY OF ALCOHOLISM

One of the difficulties in understanding and treating the alcoholic is the complexity of the problem. We probe for the reasons a person becomes an alcoholic and often overlook the fact of addiction itself. We must begin by accepting the fact that addiction to alcohol is the reason for our loved one's bondage and start the road to recovery from there.

When I was at the Open Door Mission in Omaha, the problem of alcohol addiction was being discussed in one of the group therapy classes in the New Life Program. Each of the forty-five individuals present gave a different reason for being addicted to alcohol.

"I drink because I'm lonely," one explained. "Usually when I go into a bar, it's not for liquor. I just want to find someone to talk to. But the first thing I know I've got a glass in my hand and I'm gone again."

"I used to want to be somebody and make something of my life," another told us. "But I haven't had what it takes. No matter what I try or how hard I work at it I fail. I've always been a failure. I suppose that's the way I'll always be."

"I've been a drunk for more than twenty years," still another admitted candidly. "Before I came here I didn't even try to get help. The way I saw it, there wasn't any use. A guy like me could never learn to live without alcohol."

Those three are typical alcoholics. They have their problems figured out. They reach the conclusion that it is hopeless to even try to change. They are doomed to a life of drunkenness and an early grave.

Had we accepted their reasons as the causes for their continued drinking we would have been faced with a staggering number of problems that defied solution. We would have been as helpless in our attempts to point them to lives of sobriety as they were helpless to free themselves.

But instead of accepting what they said, we confronted them with the fact that anyone can become addicted to alcohol. Then they began to understand their own behavior and see that their strange pattern of living was developed to satisfy their addictive drive. It did not necessarily come from personality defects. They saw that the hope of taking their places as useful, upright members of society was within their reach.

Many attribute alcohol addiction to some physical, moral, or psychological defect in an individual's makeup. That theory maintains that a person is an alcoholic even before he takes his first drink. Such a conclusion removes all blame from alcohol and places it on the individual. It implies that the rest of us, who are not so unfortunate, should be able to drink without any risk of running into trouble with alcohol.

WHAT CAUSES ALCOHOLISM?

The term *alcoholism* was first used by Magnus Huss and may be defined as any change in the condition of the body or in its physical or mental activities caused by ethyl alcohol or alcoholic beverages. Alcoholism is literally a poisoning by spirits.

It is the ethyl alcohol in beer, whiskey, and other liquors that causes intoxication. It is ethyl alcohol that causes addiction.

The fact that there are those who drink because of personality defects cannot be denied. Yet basic research does not hold to the premise that the psychological makeup of a man is the primary cause of his alcohol addiction.

Dr. Robert Fleming, one of the leaders in the World Health Organization, says, "Most alcoholics are not psychiatric cases: they are normal people." The conclusion reached in a fifty-six-page report issued by the World Health Organization is: "First, nobody is immune to alcoholism. Second, total abstinence is the only solution. . . . Alcohol is a poison to the nervous system. The double solubility of alcohol in water and fat enables it to invade the nerve cell. A person may become a chronic alcoholic without ever having shown symptoms of drunkenness."

Dr. Edwin H. Sunderland of Indiana University reached the same conclusion. "The alcoholic could be a sad type or a happy type, an introvert or an extrovert. In short, he could be anybody."

Alcoholism starts with the social drinking of alcoholic beverages, not with a problem personality. All alcoholic beverages—wine, beer, or whiskey—contain ethyl alcohol, a habit-forming drug. It doesn't matter which carrying agent is used; too much of any alcoholic beverage causes the same result—drunkenness.

Dr. Jorge Valles, director of the Alcoholism Unit Treatment and Research Program of the Veterans Hospital in Houston, Texas, in his book *Social Drinking and Alcoholism*, makes this statement:

> The cause of alcoholism is alcohol. For many years we have known that alcohol is the agent that produces Chronic Alcoholism. However, for one reason or another this basic fact so important to the understanding of both the disease and the patient, has been ignored or laid aside. We do not mean to be facetious when we say that there has never been a case of alcoholism recorded in which the patient had not ingested alcohol. Furthermore, the reason for a person's drinking an alcoholic beverage does not make him an alcoholic. If one needed a reason or a problem every time he reached for an alcoholic drink the number of alcoholics in our country

would be considerably less than what it is today.

He goes on to quote a statement by Drs. L. Goldberg and R. G. Bell in which they say that a person who is healthy in all respects can fall victim to the disease of alcoholism if he ingests great quantities of alcohol over a long period of time. No previous psychological or emotional disorder is necessary.

Dr. Bell also says, "Many patients who have been able to adapt physically to large quantities of alcohol and have spent their adult lives in a setting where it is customary can become seriously addicted without having been psychologically ill at the on-set of drinking."[1]

Dr. Valles identifies three steps in addiction:

1. A substance [alcohol] . . . has less effect when intake is repeated.
2. A prolonged intake.
3. The rise in the minimal effective dose.

When these factors are present addiction may result. In these cases alcoholism is due entirely to the physiological and pharmacological properties of alcohol. The psychological constitution of the victim plays no role. Entirely healthy people can become addicted to alcohol. The same applies to other poisons.[2]

Before quoting the findings of twenty two studies on the subject, covering a period from 1935-1960 (a series of studies whose conclusions are still valid), Dr. E. M. Jellinek, founder of the Yale Center of Alcohol Studies, wrote, "Most of these formulations will come as a shock to those who believe in the obsolescence of the idea of alcoholism as a true addiction and who do not recognize that alcohol itself plays more of a role in the process of alcoholism than just that of causing intoxication."

One study concluded, "The process of alcohol addic-

1. Jorge Valles, *Social Drinking and Alcoholism* (Tex.: Texas Alcohol and Narcotics Educations Council, 1965), p. 23.
2. Ibid., p. 14.

tion is comparable to the pharmacological processes operative in all drug addictions." Another added, "Loss of control over the use of alcohol, change in tolerance, a withdrawal syndrome and the relinquishing of all other interests in favor of a preoccupation with the use of alcohol are all criteria of an addiction."

Two Types of Alcoholics

Members of the Committee on Alcoholism of the American Medical Association's Council on Mental Health divided alcoholics into two groups. The first, *primary* alcoholics, are those who drink because of addiction alone. *Secondary* alcoholics are those who begin to drink compulsively because of personal problems or for physical reasons and later become addicted.

The primary alcoholic can be attracted to alcohol from the first drink and keep right on drinking until he is a slave to it.

The wife of a prominent businessman in a city in which we used to live belongs to that group. At a cocktail party she was induced to take a drink for the first time at the age of fifty-seven.

She came home and exultantly told her husband, "I didn't know what I'd been missing. I'll never be without alcohol as long as I live."

She started to drink and continued drinking compulsively. Soon she was living for the bottle, and her marriage was in shambles.

A man in Chicago tells that he was raised in a Christian home, taught Sunday school, and studied for the ministry. "You may find this hard to believe, but I had never taken a drink or smoked a cigarette until I was in my twenties. Then I took one drink and—boom! I was drunk more than I was sober. I plunged to the bottom in a matter of weeks and stumbled from one skid row to another all across the country. I lived that way for ten solid years until the Lord once more got hold of me."

The AMA report also deals with the individual who drinks regularly over a period of years until he develops such a craving for alcohol that he cannot leave it alone. He is the person who started by drinking socially.

Studies made by Jellinek conclude that addiction sets in after a period of seven years of regular drinking. Surveys made by Alcoholics Anonymous reveal that after seven to twelve years of regular drinking many drinkers become alcoholics.

Each of us has a certain capacity for ethyl alcohol without getting into trouble. But no one knows whether his capacity is as large as an oil drum or as small as a teaspoon, and he won't know until it runs over and he is an alcoholic.

A small-town businessman came to our office for help with a serious drinking problem some months ago. His wife admitted, reluctantly, that she was the one who first urged him to drink, for social reasons.

"Everyone in our crowd drank at parties and our bridge club," she said defensively. "I felt stupid asking for a Coke or Seven-Up when everyone else had a martini. So I told my husband that no harm could come from taking one drink with the others."

And she was not aware that harm was being done until, with increasing horror, she saw that her husband was addicted to alcohol.

"We live in a drinking society," said Phyllis Snyder, executive director of the Alcoholic Treatment Center in Chicago, "and therefore society is responsible for the problem involved therewith. When I was a girl, guests were usually served coffee. Now, as soon as they arrive, the host asks, 'How about a drink?' "

Pressure is constantly put upon people to drink in order to be sociable. And, with the increase of drinking, addiction increases as well.

To understand the secondary alcoholic we must understand that his problem is progressive. Jellinek describes the descent in this manner:

Alcoholism begins with occasional relief drinking while the drinker constantly needs its relief. Soon he urgently wants his first drink. Then he feels guilty and he can't discuss the problem. Memory blackouts begin and increase in frequency. Men often develop various degrees of aggressive behavior and some women act sensually. Before long the alcoholic develops work and money problems. He denies he has a problem by blaming others and rationalizing his drinking.

In this crucial phase the alcoholic avoids family and friends. Because alcohol contains empty calories he feels warm and full and therefore neglects proper food. Malnutrition sets in. His descent accelerates and the physical deterioration becomes more pronounced. Then he begins drinking with inferiors, has undefinable fears and vague spiritual desires. He hits bottom and will stay at the bottom until he admits his alcoholism and the need of help."[3]

The secondary alcoholic, according to the AMA, is an entirely different type of individual from the primary alcoholic. The secondary alcoholic is trying to escape from his personal problems by hiding in the bottle.

That category is the one into which I once fit, at least partially. I started drinking conventionally enough, using alcohol as a sales tool in the advertising and sales promotion business. When I experienced a few business reversals, I remembered the way a cocktail had relaxed me, so I began to drink for a different reason. I was tense and worried and looking for release. It wasn't long before I was addicted.

An older man we'll call John was another fellow who drank because of personal problems. He didn't drink at all until after his wife died. Left with four small children and a limited income that made it all but impossible to hire a housekeeper, he saw no way to escape—except through alcohol. It had a numbing effect on his mind and made it possible for him to forget his troubles for a few hours. If he

3. Ibid.

got drunk enough he could temporarily forget that his children were in foster homes.

John's bouts with the bottle only increased his problems, which in turn caused him to drink more often. First he lost his job. Next he lost his home. Then, in addition to his personal problems, before he even realized what was happening, he was caught in the savage vise of alcohol addiction.

The guilt complex can play a big part in sending the secondary alcoholic on the downward road of alcoholism. One young man who came for help admitted that he was an alcoholic and wanted to be set free. He had a good background and was well educated, with outstanding ability as a private secretary. He had held such a position with a leading businessman and civic leader. Under the influence of alcohol this young man had committed a crime and spent two years in prison. Because of his ability and fine family background everyone wanted to help him make a new start. But he could not maintain any degree of success for any length of time. Just as he would reach his goal, he would go on another drunk. Prayerful study of his problem showed that he had a guilt complex he could not overcome. He felt that he did not deserve success because he had disgraced his family.

Vernon E. Johnson, well-known author of *I'll Quit Tomorrow* and a number of articles on alcoholism, states, "The most startling observation has been that alcoholism can not exist unless there is a conflict between the values and the behavior of the drinker."

Roy E. Hatfield writes in *Christianity Today*, "Today social drinking has become quite acceptable in many segments of the evangelical church. Forty eight percent of the Baptist community, for example, use alcoholic beverages. But it is interesting to note that 18% of those got into trouble. The reason is probably guilt. Baptists and others from similar backgrounds are more likely to get into difficulty simply because they suffer more guilt when they use alcohol."[4]

Earlier I made reference to the fact that I was a secondary alcoholic. I drank socially in connection with my business but had feelings of guilt because of it. When I was a child I was taught that drinking was not proper for me. My father never drank. In fact, he wore a white ribbon he had received from the Women's Christian Temperance Union when he was a small boy for pledging never to drink. He kept that commitment and never did.

I was raised in the Methodist church during the days when drinking alcoholic beverages was taboo for members of that denomination. I heard frequent messages on the value of abstinence. So when I started drinking I knew it was wrong and that my behavior would not be accepted by the people I grew up with.

Guilt plays a big part in leading evangelical church members into trouble when they start drinking socially. In general, once they start drinking such people fall into the grip of alcoholism much more easily than those from other backgrounds.

It is not always a psychological problem that gets the secondary alcoholic in trouble. With some it may be a physical problem.

A nervous, sensitive person, Steve stuttered terribly. As an impressionable boy, however, he discovered that it didn't hurt so much if people laughed at him after he had had a drink or two. In fact, liquor loosed his inhibitions until he could make sport of the infirmity himself. His drinking soon caused addiction, which was aggravated while he served a stretch in the army during the Korean War. He lost his wife and family and everything he considered worth living for and continued to drink heavily until ethyl alcohol finally took his life.

Another such individual came into my office and ad-

---

4. Roy E. Hatfield, "Closet Alcoholics in the Church," *Christianity Today,* 18 August 1981, p. 28.

mitted miserably, "Liquor has complete control over me."

"What is your problem as far as alcohol is concerned?" I asked him.

"That's just it. As far as I know I don't have any personal problems that would cause me to drink the way I do. My business is good, and we're not in any financial difficulties. I have a fine wife and family, and we get along very well together. I don't have any problems I can think of," he said sheepishly, "except that I can't sleep at night. I've got undulant fever, and insomnia seems to go with it."

Although he didn't realize it, that was his problem. He wouldn't be able to sleep for several nights in a row. Tension would begin to build. Then he would drink so that he could sleep. He soon became addicted. The weakness that induced him to drink in the first place was soon succeeded by the greater weakness of his insatiable, acquired thirst for ethyl alcohol.

WHO ARE AMERICA'S ALCOHOLICS?

Depending on whose statistics we read, the number of known alcoholics in the United States ranges anywhere from ten to fifteen million. Half of that number are women, and more than 95 percent still have their jobs and families.

The National Council on Alcoholism in 1981 stated that 10 percent of America's work force has drinking problems that affect job performance. Drinking workers make poor decisions, spoil materials, or don't show up at all. Ironically, many of them are relatively high-ranking employees with twenty years or more on the job.

Dr. Eric D. Davis, Medical Director of Seattle's Shadle Hospital, adds this comment: "The vast majority of alcohol addicts have families, homes and steady employment." As a matter of record, only 3 to 5 percent of the known alcoholics in America ever reach the skid-row level.

The amount of drinking done by women has risen rapidly in recent years. Cocktail parties are taking the place of afternoon coffee parties, and liquor is more and more often served at bridge clubs. Some drink because they have a great deal of leisure time and are bored. Some drink because it has become the thing to do in their circle of society. Whatever the reason, addiction starts with social drinking. The results are exactly what one would expect. An article in the January 1985 issue of *Reader's Digest* quotes a Gallop Poll that found a slight downward trend in the amount of drinking that is being done in the United States. Sixty-five percent indicated that they drank wine, beer, or hard liquor at least once in a while. A 1977 poll stated that 71 percent interviewed said that they drank at least occasionally.

In addition, 29 percent of those who admitted to drinking said they were drinking less than they were five years ago, whereas only 11 percent said they were drinking more. In the 18-to-29 age group, however, a disturbing 21 percent said they were drinking more.

In the same poll, 81 percent of those interviewed said they regarded alcohol abuse as a major problem and wanted the government to do more in the way of controlling it.

Whether these changes in the drinking habits of Americans is an indication of a long-term trend is difficult to know. It could well be caused by the public outcry against drunken driving and might reverse itself when the present push to get drunks out of cars and off our highways begins to run out of steam. We should be much in prayer that the American people finally wake up to the devastating effects of alcohol on us as individuals and as a nation.

· DEFINITION AND EFFECTS OF INTOXICATION

There was a time when an individual was judged to be intoxicated or sober by his ability to walk a straight line and to speak distinctly. That is no longer the case.

Dr. Harvey Wiley said it this way: "A man can be intoxicated without tottering or without disclosing in any way to the ordinary sense the fact that he is intoxicated."

Dr. Yendell Henderson, professor of applied psychology at Yale University, said, "Since the introduction of the automobile, however, the definition (of intoxication) may be changed to that which appreciably impairs the ability of a man or a woman to drive an automobile with safety to the general public."

Dr. Morris Fishbein wrote his own convictions on the same subject in the AMA Journal. "Just a drink or two and the safe driver is turned into a reckless traffic menace."

There is good reason for this. Ethyl alcohol, when taken into the body, goes almost immediately into the bloodstream and up to the brain. It begins to affect the cortex of the brain, the location of higher brain centers that have to do with memory, conscience, and judgment. The anesthetic effect of alcohol slows man's reactions measurably. It decreases his ability to judge distances and to tell the difference between visual and auditory stimuli.

It adversely affects skilled performance. A crack rifle team discovered that as little as one glass of beer materially lowered their scores.

But that is not all. Ethyl alcohol makes it more difficult to memorize data and solve problems.

Those who drink will argue that drinking may affect the driving ability of others, but it does not affect them. But tests conducted by the University of Washington School of Medicine revealed that only 3/100 percent of ethyl alcohol in the blood stream lowered a person's driving efficiency by 25 percent. Two cans of beer or their equivalent will produce this effect in the individual of average size. Increase the alcoholic intake to six cans of beer, and the individual will have 10/100 percent alcohol in the blood stream; his ability to drive will be retarded by 85 percent.

K. M. Magruder wrote in *Alcohol and Drug Education:*

North Carolina sells liquor only through state-controlled stores. Individual counties decide by referendum which alcoholic beverages will be available in their counties, or if none will be sold at all. Five different possibilities of availability of alcoholic beverages were possible in the study. It was found there was almost a straight line relationship between mortality from alcohol-related diseases and the liberality of the law governing the availability in counties. The finding was in spite of the fact that it is no great trouble for individuals to go across county lines to buy alcohol. It is interesting that the availability of alcoholic beverages increases the amount of alcoholism in a given area and also increases the death rate from alcohol-related diseases.[5]

Dr. Gordon L. Addington, in his book *The Christian and Social Drinking*, verifies earlier findings regarding the parallel between increased drinking and the increase of alcohol-related diseases.

His research reveals that the mortality from alcohol disorders has shown a marked increase from 1964 to 1976.

> The disorders are defined as Alcohol Psychosis. Alcoholism and Alcohol-caused cirrhosis of the liver. The latter shows a 46% mortality increase for white males, and a 107% increase for non-white males. The mortality increase for white females has increased 36% with an increase of 76% for non-white females. . . .
>
> Until recently it was assumed that the deleterius or harmful effects of alcohol were largely due to nutritional deficiencies. Those who drank heavily were notoriously careless about their diet and neglected proper nutrition. During the past several years, however, it has become clear that alcohol itself is a toxin to many body organs and that proper and adequate nutrition does not protect the drinking individual from the effects of alcohol.[6]

The *Alcoholism Report* published in December of

5. K. M. Magruder, "The Association the Alcoholism Mortality with Legal Availability of Alcoholic Beverages," Alcohol and Drug Education, 1976.
6. Gordon L. Addington, *The Christian and Social Drinking* (Minneapolis: Free Church Publications, 1984).

1983 made this startling comment in reviewing the Consumer's Federation of America's report:

> Alcohol was third, behind automobiles and cigarettes in the top ten most hazardous of consumer products. Millions of Americans abuse or are addicted to alcohol. This abuse is a major cause of tens of thousands of deaths and millions of injuries that occur each year in accidents involving automobiles, boats and weapons. Moreover, heavy drinking is as important a cause of disease as cigarette smoking. Medical researchers have directly linked heavy consumption of alcohol to heart disease, hepatitis, cirrhosis of the liver, and to cancer of the mouth, esophagus, larnyx, liver and other organs.
>
> Even small amounts of alcohol during pregnancy can be detrimental to the unborn baby. Women who have two standard drinks per day during pregnancy often give birth to smaller children. Significant increases in spontaneous miscarriages are noted in women who have as little as two drinks twice a week. Alcohol consumption during pregnancy can also cause physical and mental birth defects.
>
> The economic costs of alcohol abuse are also significant. Medical bills, time missed from work, property damage, and other associated costs totaled a hundred billion dollars in 1982. In the United States only heart and cardiovascular diseases exceeded alcohol abuse in total economic cost. In addition, alcohol is a major factor in crime. Eighty six percent of homicides involve alcohol. Seventy nine percent of assaults, seventy two percent of robberies, fifty percent of rapes and fifty percent of automobile accidents.

The Bible clearly teaches that the problem of alcoholism lies with the product, not just the individual. "Who has woe? Who has sorrow? Who has strife? Who has complaints? Who has needless bruises? Who has bloodshot eyes? Those who linger over wine, who go to sample bowls of mixed wine. Do not gaze at wine when it is red, when it sparkles in the cup, when it goes down smoothly! In the end it bites like a snake and poisons like a viper" (Proverbs 23:29-32, NIV*).

*New International Version.

TWO

THE SEVEN STEPS TO ALCOHOLISM
(STEPS 1-4)

Before it is possible to help the alcoholic, it is necessary to understand him. We must remember that all alcoholism starts with social drinking.

"Though I know you don't drink, even socially," a medical doctor told a friend of ours, "you may be an alcoholic."

Although we might question the doctor's terminology, what he said could be true. The fellow may be psychotic. He may be neurotic. He may have some other type of personality difficulty that would make him particularly vulnerable to alcohol addiction. He might have inherited a family weakness that would make social drinking exceedingly dangerous for him. He might even be the type who has only to take one drink to ignite the flames of thirst that would destroy him.

But until he takes that first drink he is as safe from alcoholic addiction as Adam and Eve were safe from death before they ate of the forbidden fruit.

There are seven distinct steps downward from sobriety to alcoholism and complete deterioration of the human mind and body. In the life of any given individual some of the steps may be blurred and run together, but careful examination will reveal each of them. We will cover the first four in this chapter and the final three in the next.

These steps can be warning signals—stop signs in the

progressive downward march to alcoholism and destruction—or signposts to mark the distance a man has yet to go. Unfortunately, his loved ones cannot decide which they will be. Only the individual can make such a decision.

SOCIAL DRINKING

The first step is social drinking. Practically without exception, people take their first drink because someone offers them one.

A few years ago young people began to feel the pressure to drink when they reached high school or college. Today it often begins in junior high, where increasing numbers think they have to have beer to enjoy a party. During the past school year, a small midwestern town was stunned when thirty-eight students attending a school-sponsored junior high dance were caught drinking. About the same time, in a television documentary on teenage drinking, an eleven-year-old girl in an alcoholic treatment program told of her experience with alcohol dependency.

School authorities are usually aware of the problem but in many cases have to battle the parents in order to do anything about it. A case came to our attention concerning beer drinking at a junior high dance. The school principal expelled the students involved and, among other things, forced them to take an alcoholic evaluation test before readmitting them to class. The only opposition to that decision came from prominent parents who were outraged that their children would be treated so shamefully.

Getting alcohol is no problem for most youngsters. They don't have to go to someone on a street corner to buy what they want. Many get their first drink from the refrigerator at home and most of their beer from their parents' supply in the basement or garage.

Mothers and fathers are often so concerned about marijuana, cocaine, and other drugs that they are almost relieved to learn that their children are only dabbling with alcohol. They may not realize that alcohol is also a drug, with the potential to destroy the lives of the unwary, and in a number of ways is more dangerous than the drugs every parent fears.

We often fail to consider that the effect of alcohol on an individual has a direct relationship to his body weight. A can of beer will have far less effect on a 225-pound man than it will on a boy or girl of 90 pounds. Even a small amount of alcohol can have a devastating effect on a child.

By the time many reach high school they are already on the road to problem drinking.

"I started hitting the bottle when I was fourteen," a Canadian friend told me. "Before the year was out I was a full-fledged alcoholic. I'd lie and steal to get another drink."

When I was speaking in Pennsylvania not long ago it was suggested by the church group sponsoring my appearance that I visit the local schools. They were able to get me into the junior high, but the high school principal was so afraid of violating the law regarding separation of church and state that he refused to allow me to speak to his assembly. When one of the prominent women in the community heard about that, she phoned to talk to him about it.

"I'd like very much to have him come," he said, as soon as he learned the purpose of the call. "I had a chilling thing happen just now. A mother just left my office with a ninth-grade girl who was stoned out of her mind on alcohol. The teacher brought her to me in that condition, and I had to phone the mother and have her come to get the girl."

A high school teacher from another part of the United States told me, "I have had kids come into my classes who were so drunk they scarcely knew where they were. We try to do something about it, but often they are problem drinkers, and we have no way of helping them except to urge their parents to get professional help for them."

In a small Nebraska town the inevitable round of graduation parties was held. A seventeen-year-old girl got drunk and went home with a girl friend. The next morning she was found in the bathtub, dead by drowning. Accidental deaths of graduating students in automobile accidents are common across the country and often take the lives of the innocent as well.

In colleges and universities, drinking becomes a way of life. Schools that try to control alcohol in the dorms have been forced to set up security guards in an attempt to keep it out. The pressure to drink socially is sometimes irresistible even to those initially determined not to participate in parties and drinking bouts. And in exceptional cases, even physical pressure has been used. At a state school in Nebraska, classmates of a polio victim in a wheelchair wrestled him to the floor and tried to force liquor down his throat.

A young student nurse told friends of ours, "You should have been with us two nights ago. We had another keg party. When all the beer was gone we started making the rounds of the bars. Had a drink in every one we stopped at. I don't remember what time we got home. But, oh, my head!" She held her head with both hands and smiled as though a hangover was something to be proud of.

"You have to drink when you go to a party," a university sophomore said to me. "Everybody does."

The pattern for gracious living set by adults has filtered down to their children. An evening cannot be a success without the hospitality hour. At many parties the pressure to get everyone to drink is so great it seems imperative that everyone have a glass in his hand, even if it only contains ginger ale. For some reason drinkers feel uncomfortable if someone is present who isn't drinking.

"I don't know why people will come to our neighborhood parties and be so smug they won't drink," a woman complained in a newspaper advice column. "It wouldn't hurt them to take just one cocktail."

A young Christian couple attached to the United States Embassy in Spain were at a reception for a foreign dignitary. The time came for refreshments, and the wife turned down the cocktail she was offered. The woman behind her was horrified.

"You have to take it!" she whispered. "It's protocol! It's protocol!"

The Christian had strong convictions against drinking and refused. Her would-be mentor was deeply offended. Only intervention by the ambassador stopped an ugly confrontation, so determined was the older woman that her Christian counterpart have a drink.

"The more education an American has the more likely he is to drink," says Robert W. Jones, assistant director of the Center of Alcohol Studies at Rutgers University. "More than half the people with only an elementary education drink. Approximately 70 percent of those with high school educations drink, while the percentage is somewhat greater among college graduates."

The liquor industry spends millions of dollars a year in advertising. Their purpose is to cloak their product with some semblance of respectability and to foster the notion that successful social occasions call for alcohol. Their propaganda campaign has been very successful through the years. More and more evangelical Christians find themselves relaxing their opposition to social drinking and are adopting drinking habits that closely resemble those of American society in general. Consequently we are seeing increasing numbers of Christians falling into alcohol addiction.

No one thinks he will become a slave to alcohol. The social drinker is determined not to drink so much that he staggers or makes a fool of himself or is a risk behind the steering wheel. He doesn't intend to make liquor the first love of his life—to the exclusion of his family, his friends, and his job. "I've seen it happen to others," he reasons, "but it is not going to happen to me." He is too smart—too much in control of himself—to let liquor master him. But, like 99 percent of all alcoholics, the chances are that he will not even recognize the danger signals until it is too late.

Although social drinking is the first step to alcoholism, another even more insidious danger is the idea rapidly taking hold of more and more people that to demonstrate hospitality an alcoholic beverage must be served. Social drinking is the snare that traps many individuals who have fought their way back to sobriety.

A man we'll call Pete was such a person. The path had been long and difficult for him, but at last he reached the place where he could stay sober He won back his wife and family, got a good job, bought a new home, and was once more getting ahead. It had been five years since he had a drink.

Then his wife went to visit her mother. While he was at home alone the people in the block had a housewarming for a new couple who had moved into the neighborhood. Anxious to be hospitable, the newcomers brought up a case of beer from the basement.

At first Pete hesitated. He knew he shouldn't drink, that it was dangerous for him to do so. But how could he explain all of that to complete strangers? Rather than give them the sordid story of his drinking days he took a beer.

He was determined to handle it, but the fires of alcoholism had not been put out. They had only been banked within him and were still smoldering. The taste of alcohol in that single glass of beer was enough to catch fire and send the flames racing out of control.

Although five years had elapsed, he started to drink again. You know the rest of the story. He lost his job, his home, his family, and once more hit skid row—all because someone offered him a social drink and he was too embarrassed to turn it down.

Dependent Drinking

The second step toward alcoholism is dependent drinking. The alcoholic's reasons for drinking change subtly but perceptibly. No longer does he drink only when he has guests or is a guest himself. He becomes either a habitual drinker or a dependent drinker. Which type he is depends upon his reason for drinking in the first place. It depends upon whether he could be considered by the AMA classification as a primary or secondary alcoholic.

The habit drinker is the person who is just beginning to feel the powerful, insistent tug of addiction. He mixes a drink when he comes home from the office or after dinner while reading or watching television. If it is a woman, she will do the same when she gets home from work or when she sits down for a few minutes to rest from housework or the constant pressure of caring for the children. Such people are usually not even aware that they are developing a growing habit of drinking that can lead them to alcoholism.

"It became a regular ritual with us," said one young woman whose marriage was threatened because her husband was an alcoholic. "At first, we only drank socially. Then about once or twice a week Paul would mix us a drink as soon as he got home from work. It wasn't long until he went from the hall closet where he hung his coat directly to the bottle in the refrigerator. Even then, we didn't think anything about it."

The story of Michele, told in the November 1981 issue of *Moody Monthly*, reveals that this can happen even to a fine Christian young woman. Michele, a member of an evangelical church, was promoted to the position of sales manager at the company where she worked. The opportunities to drink looked inviting, and she began to drink socially.

At first she was sure it helped business. Her clients seemed more relaxed when she drank with them, and she thought it helped in making sales. It wasn't long, however, until she was unable to control her drinking. In a few months she came to church under the influence of alcohol. She had never intended it to go that far, but it did.

The *dependent drinker* turns to beverage alcohol when things start to build up; when the problems he faces get to be too great for him. His boss chews him out on the job; he loses a big contract; his wife wants to spend more than he thinks they can afford on new furniture; or a bill collector gets nasty. So he drinks. It helps him to forget what has happened. The disappointments and frustrations don't seem so great under the temporary glow produced by alcohol.

I know quite a lot about that sort of drinking. I used to do my share of it.

If something happened that disturbed me or made me angry I'd head for the nearest bar or package store. The bottle didn't solve a single problem, but that didn't keep me from running to it for solace. Nor did I face the fact that I always felt worse and less able to cope with life when the effect of the liquor wore off. Even though at that time my chief compulsion to drink came from the pressures I faced, I was becoming addicted to ethyl alcohol. And, like the habit drinker, I didn't realize it.

There is actually little difference between the habit drinker and the dependent drinker. Both are in the early stages of alcohol addiction.

PREALCOHOLIC PHASE

The third step is the prealcoholic phase. Here again the step is sharply defined. Well entrenched now as a regular drinker of alcoholic beverages, the individual begins to drink hastily. He gulps his drinks and drinks on the sly so his family and friends won't know about it. At the party such an individual volunteers to be bartender.

On one pretext or another the person in the prealcoholic phase will manage to get into the kitchen where the drinks are mixed. His own glass is always filled, or he'll make and gulp down an extra drink every time someone else comes for a refill. Although until this point he has seldom shown the effects of drinking too much, such an individual now begins to reveal evidences of intoxication at otherwise quiet cocktail parties.

"I'll never forget the night I first realized my husband

actually drank too much," a distraught wife confided to me. "We had gone to a New Year's Eve party at a friend's home. The other guests had two or three drinks, but Herman must have had one every time he went to the kitchen. He made a fool of himself and fell on the floor twice before I got him home and in bed."

He felt terrible about his exhibition and swore off drinking—for a whole week.

"After that," she went on, "it seemed that at every third or fourth cocktail party we went to he got in that condition." Tears came to her eyes. "He certainly isn't like the man I married."

She spoke the truth. He wasn't the same man she had married twelve or fourteen years before. A change in his personality had set in. He had begun to develop what is known as an alcoholic personality.

"He never used to lie to me," she went on. "It didn't make any difference what had happened, or how angry the truth made me, he had never lied to me—but I began to catch him telling things that weren't true. I soon discovered that now I couldn't believe anything he said."

He would call her, very apologetically, to tell her that a deal came up unexpectedly, demanding his immediate attention.

"I don't know what's the matter with people that they can't conduct business at a decent hour, but a good customer called a few minutes ago, insisting that I make a presentation to him and the assistant purchasing agent before they go to New York tonight. I tried every way I know to get out of it, but it's either do as they say or lose the order."

When he told such lies, he sounded very convincing. Even when he would be gone all night, he had a logical reason for his predicament. One time his car was supposed to have broken down, and he was so far out in the country he had to wait until morning to get help. Another time, he told his secretary to phone his wife that he'd been called to a neighboring town unexpectedly and probably wouldn't be able to get home that night. His excuses were very plausible and persuasive.

Even in the prealcoholic phase the individual becomes an accomplished liar. Deceit and lying become a way of life to keep the family and employer from knowing that he is drinking more and more.

This is something you must remember if you are dealing with an alcoholic. It doesn't make any difference who the person is—whether it is a man or woman, rich or poor, intelligent or slow, important or unimportant—he becomes an accomplished liar. He is able to look you straight in the eye and speak with the tones of one taking a solemn oath without uttering a single word of truth.

PROBLEM DRINKING

Problem drinking is the fourth step. The prealcoholic begins to lose control of his drinking habits. Before he could control the time he started to drink and the time he stopped. Now he has reached the stage when he can control the time he starts to drink but can't stop when he wants to. The fires of alcohol addiction begin to flame higher, and he can no longer quench his thirst. He begins to go on weekend drunks.

A fellow we'll call Ken was like this. A near genius mechanically, he and a partner had developed a piece of equipment that could be used by large contractors. They began to manufacture it and set out to contact prospective customers.

"Ken would spend weeks setting up appointments," a disturbed employee confided. "He'd take money he needed badly and go to a place like Chicago or Philadelphia or New York to see important buyers. Then, to bolster his courage he'd take a drink. He'd get stinking drunk and lie in his hotel room for two or three days without seeing anyone he made the trip to see."

Ross had a similar problem. He was the vice president in charge of sales for a nationally distributed product. It was his responsibility to train and encourage district sales managers across the country. All such meetings included a hospitality hour, which he would arrange and supervise.

At first he was able to take a drink or leave it alone. He saw social drinking as an effective sales tool, not a personal threat. But it wasn't long before he was drinking habitually and was only a step from the prealcoholic phase. When he came to that phase, he drank more than anyone else at the parties. Then, without quite realizing what had happened, he could no longer stop drinking when he wanted to.

He would arrange for the area sales force to come into a central location and have every intention of carrying out the elaborate program he had set up. But at the hospitality hour he would drink so much he was unable to conduct the meeting. He not only made a fool of himself, but he also ruined his sales meetings. After two or three warnings, he lost his position—one that paid him an impressive annual salary.

The loss of his job meant real problems for Ross at home and with his friends. Typical of the problem drinker progressing downward, his personality began to change. He became dependent upon others as fears and anxiety set in. A great change came into his life. Fighting his way to the top of his department, he had been a dynamic individual. Supremely confident of his own abilities he had waded into any task, certain that he would be able to see it through to a successful conclusion. Now the qualities that had first attracted the attention of the top management and gained him rapid advancement gradually faded away. He was hesitant and unsure of himself, a shadow of what he once was. Both he and his family suffered.

In the past thirty years I have received many letters from problem drinkers and their families. Even since I retired from the City Mission in Lincoln, Nebraska, I continue to get a number of letters each week.

"I attend church every Sunday and have a regular Bible study once a week," a lady wrote from upstate New York.

"I'm thirty-six years old, have three beautiful children and a wonderful husband. I should be one of the happiest women in our community, but I have one problem. I find myself drinking at home alone for no apparent reason.

"My husband is a good man but is not a Christian. We keep praying. I have prayed and prayed but somehow the devil comes in, and I have one drink after another until I feel good and nothing bothers me.

"My two older children go to Sunday school, Christian camp, and this year they will be attending a Christian school. No one knows anything about my problem because I'm very careful about my drinking. So I go on with my housework, but meanwhile I have already had four or five drinks. It tears me apart inside. I'm sick with guilt. We live comfortably, and I have everything a person could want or hope for, but I am alone—fighting!"

Another man, who became a problem drinker, frequently went to bridge or cocktail parties with his wife on Saturday nights. Once in a while they went somewhere with friends for an entire weekend. But when they did, the husband's drinking soon caused serious difficulties.

"I can't understand it," his wife said. "When Don takes a drink he can't stop. Last Saturday night he got drunk and wasn't sober until Monday morning."

It wasn't long until he was staying drunk until well into the next week. His wife felt that she had to cover up for him in order to help him keep from losing his job.

"Don's sick this morning," she would tell his supervisor. "He has the flu." Or, "There's something wrong with his back. I've been trying to get him to see the doctor."

A once competent, self-assured workman who was conscientious about his job, Don depended on his wife to lie for him when he got drunk. He looked to her to help him keep the truth from his employer. He began to realize that he had a problem with alcohol, and he was caught between savage fear and pride on one hand and the gradual realization of his true situation on the other.

It is at this point that the problem drinker experiences

great torment. He goes on a business trip, starts to drink, and can't stop. He becomes dead drunk and only vaguely remembers anything that happened.

I shall never forget how I felt when I woke up in a Midwest city one time in this stage of alcoholism. The past several days were a complete blank. I had no idea of what had happened, except that I had written checks I didn't have the money to cover.

I began to see that I was a liar, a cheat, a thief, and a drunkard. I wouldn't have admitted any of those things to anyone else, but deep in my own heart I knew they were true. It was a frightening experience.

"If I could just take care of the immediate problem," I reasoned, "I can handle things from here on. If I can get enough money to make those checks good, I won't get myself into a mess like that again." Yet the gnawing realization that I was helpless against the fierce thirst that was taking hold of me was a real torment.

Frantically I began to search for answers, all the while fearful that people would find me out. A short time later I went to a psychiatrist, desperate for help. But pride wouldn't let me admit that I couldn't take care of myself and my own problems. Pride wouldn't let me acknowledge to anyone that I had a problem with alcohol.

From this point, the alcoholic's downward progression becomes almost a blur. He is on a collision course with disaster but doesn't know what to do about it.

THREE

THE SEVEN STEPS TO ALCOHOLISM (STEPS 5-7)

THE DROPOVER POINT

The fifth step is the dropover into alcoholism. Until the individual reaches this point the problem drinker is able to maintain a somewhat normal life. But now his growing addiction to alcohol is affecting members of his family, his friends, and his associates.

He reaches the place where his entire life is centered on one thing and only one thing—getting another drink. He can no longer control either the time he starts drinking or the time he stops.

Even though he may want—desperately—to keep from drinking, his very being screams for the alcohol to which he has become addicted. He starts to drink because he cannot help it and continues in long periods of intoxication because he can no longer keep from it.

His body has built up a dependence upon alcohol that can no longer be denied. His entire existence becomes a battle to satisfy this insatiable craving. He becomes crafty almost to the point of animal cunning.

One alcoholic I know had a kennel of hunting dogs in his backyard. Let the dogs bark, which they usually did several times during an evening, and he would have to go out to see what was wrong. It was a very convenient arrangement for a man whose wife watched him closely in an effort to keep him from drinking. He had bottles stashed in the garage, in a pair of breast waders hanging in the back entry way, and in a pair of boots in the back of his closet. He could go anywhere on his property and never be more than thirty feet from a quick drink.

After his conversion to Christ and complete deliverance from the power of alcohol he told me that he was constantly finding hidden bottles that he had forgotten about.

"For six months after I quit drinking," he said, "we kept turning up liquor every time we moved a piece of canvas or opened a tool box or cleaned the garage. In my drinking days I was desperately afraid I would need a drink and not be able to get one."

Like my friend, the alcoholic finally reaches the place where most of his waking moments are spent thinking about alcohol. An alcoholic's cunning is boundless when it comes to working things out so he's always got a bottle close by when he needs it.

Another characteristic of the dropover into alcoholism is the individual's attitude toward his job. The average alcoholic is an exceptional workman. Whatever his responsibilities, they will be satisfactorily carried out.

Strangely enough, this also is a part of the pattern of alcoholism. The alcoholic may or may not be ambitious or conscientious when sober. But now his motive for working begins to change. He strives to do good work out of fear.

In the back of his mind he knows that, sooner or later, he is going to get drunk and not be able to get back to work on Monday or Tuesday. He's afraid that when the inevitable happens, he'll be let go—unless he has made an outstanding work record. So he works as hard as he can to make himself so valuable that his employer won't fire him.

There is another fear that motivates him. He knows that when he has been on drunks before, he has done things that he would never have done had he been sober. Perhaps he wrote bad checks or gambled or walked off without paying a hotel bill or had a close brush with the law. He thinks that by working hard enough—or if he is a salesman and has a high enough record of sales—the company will stand by him. If they like him well enough, they may advance him enough money to get things straightened out.

The alcoholic, you must remember, is cunning. He's always thinking ahead. He's always trying to prepare for the unexpected. He realizes his own weaknesses, although he won't admit them, and is constantly trying to hedge against getting himself into a corner.

We often found this trait among the men at the mission. An employer who hired a person from us usually got the best dishwasher or ditchdigger or dockman he ever had. The alcoholic often works hard without complaining and does his work so well his employer can't help being favorably impressed. But soon the reason for his hard work is revealed. After a few days he will go to the boss's office with a plausible story about needing money.

"I haven't been able to take care of my room rent," he will lie, "and the landlady has given me until tonight to get the money. I wonder if I could get a little advance on my wages."

The employer is usually so glad to have him he doesn't mind letting him have a few dollars. With money in his pocket, the fellow almost runs over somebody getting to the nearest bar, where he proceeds to get drunk. That's the last his new employer ever sees of him.

Although the individual in this stage works well, his motives are entirely selfish. All his thoughts and desires are directed toward getting another drink. In this phase of his downward trend we see the complete change in his personality.

When a person is in the prealcoholic phase he starts lying. When he becomes a problem drinker he begins to develop a dependence upon other people and is beset by the torment of fear and anxiety. He is but a short step away from alcoholism. When he drops over into alcoholism, his personality change is complete.

He not only lies and deceives everyone around him, but he also becomes self-centered and antisocial. He doesn't want to be around people—especially strangers. He would rather miss a meal than sit down with others and will often keep crackers and cheese or canned food in his room so he can eat alone.

The alcoholic won't make decisions. He becomes dependent upon his spouse, his family, and perhaps the entire community.

But, paradoxically, the alcoholic is proud—so proud that he or she will cling to any illusion that will keep people from finding out what he is really like.

Not all pride is bad, but the pride of an alcoholic is a deceitful thing. It makes him critical of everyone around him. He is close to being a perfectionist when it comes to other people. If they don't come up to the high standards he has set for them, he will be deeply upset. A recovering alcoholic may use the failures of others as an excuse for going back to his old way of life.

A woman from Massachusetts wrote me, "I went to AA for my drinking problem. And, because I wanted to keep on drinking, I began to find fault with everyone I associated with. I even found fault with the meetings. Because of that I had an excuse to continue drinking for several more years. Finally I understood why I was like I was and really found peace. The matter of looking at everyone and saying, 'You don't live up to my standards,' kept me from staying sober. In short, my pride kept me drinking."

Not long ago I was asked to counsel with a young man who had a problem with alcoholic pride. Five years before, he had been sober. Then things didn't go right for him. People didn't cooperate. He attended a church meeting, and people got up to give their testimonies.

"I could look at them and see that they couldn't possibly be like they said they were," he said. "I was so disgusted with their hypocrisy that I went back to drinking."

False pride and a judgmental attitude cause men and women like this young man to revert to the bottle. They secretly want an excuse. Now they have it. Other people have failed them, so their drinking isn't their own fault.

The alcoholic man is often too proud to allow his wife and children to draw relief of any kind, yet he may be very willing to live off his wife's earnings.

The wife of an alcoholic shoe salesman came to see me. She mentioned, among other things, the matter of her working. "We have four small children, and I feel I should be home with them. We could live quite comfortably on my husband's income, but he flies into a rage if I even mention giving up my job and staying home."

The man wanted his wife to keep a job because he had the nagging fear that one day his drinking would lead him into financial trouble and he would need her income to fall back on.

Another young man was even more dependent on his wife. Acute alcoholism took his life, eventually, but while he lived he was satisfied to let his wife—the mother of two small children—work to support the family and him.

In this phase of his descent into alcoholism the individual will probably lose his job because of his drinking. And often it won't be the last job his drinking will cost him.

The person in an average home situation is apt to develop a dependency upon the family. The homeless individual often develops a dependency on society.

One skid-row character in a Midwestern city spent 312 days of one year in jail. The charges against him were all the same—drunkenness. For him, jail was a way of life. It meant warmth, food, and a place to sleep at night—a measure of security.

For other alcoholics, the cycle is more complex, but it is essentially the same. They go from the jail to the hospital to the rescue mission to an alcoholic rehabilitation center and back to jail again.

The matter of the alcoholic's dependence upon others presents one of the most difficult and serious problems a counselor or family faces in working with the alcoholic. Dependence on others must be broken before the alcoholic can be helped.

CHRONIC ALCOHOLISM

Whereas the plunge from problem drinking to alcoholism is sudden and marked, the drift into the sixth step, chronic alcoholism, is gradual. After losing one job because of his drinking, the individual gets another. For a time all seems to go well. Then his drinking puts him out of work once more.

Tom was like that. An expert in the field of electronics, he was able to get work quite easily. He drifted from Kansas to Minnesota to Florida and back to Kansas on one job after another, taking his family with him. Each new start looked promising. In each job he was given advancements and raises for the excellence of his work. He was finally fired from each job for the same reason—his excessive drinking.

Whenever he took a job in a new community, he was determined things were going to be different. He had left all of his old friends behind. He wasn't going to run with a drinking crowd anymore. And for a while he would do better, but he always began to drink again. He drank away a good home and furniture and a late-model car. The last move he and his wife made, they had enough money for a bus ticket halfway across the country to a place where he was going to make another new start. All the clothes they owned were in a single suitcase.

Tom was very much like an engineer I knew who was very competent and could find work with ease. Even after he got to drinking so heavily he lost his job, some other company was always glad to hire him. Finally, however, the entire engineering profession put a black mark against him. Knowing he was a poor work risk, management refused to hire him anywhere in his chosen profession.

He had something else to fall back on, however. As a young man in school he had worked for an uncle who was a caterer. When engineering jobs were no longer available to him, he became a cook, an expert baker, and a kitchen manager. He would work in a cafe or bakery until the owner got tired of his drunkenness and fired him. Since there is always a shortage of cooks and bakers, he could move on, finding work enough to provide him with a room and another bottle. All the while the bands of alcohol addiction were becoming tighter.

At this stage of chronic alcoholism, the individual's family and friends have usually become so disgusted and heartsick they have finally turned against him. He is very much alone.

The pattern continues with long periods of intoxication, which usually end in delirium tremens. By this time he is no stranger to the inside of jails and has a resigned, passive attitude toward being arrested, as though there is no shame involved. While his twisted pride remains, his self-respect is gone. It is during this phase that he will probably be hospitalized for the first time because of his drinking.

Before we moved to Lincoln, Nebraska, in the late sixties all my experience had been in treating the male alcoholic. In Lincoln, however, there was a large family program where we were able to deal not only with men who were problem alcoholics but with women alcoholics and with families that were deteriorating because of alcohol. The same pattern showed itself in women alcoholics that I had seen in men.

Women alcoholics often humiliate themselves much more than men in the methods they use to finance their drinking. As a result, they may carry an additional load of guilt along with the other problems that men carry.

It seems more difficult to reach a woman in that condition and help her realize that the power of God can lift her up. We could use the words Christ said to the woman taken in adultery (John 8:). "Where are your accusers? Neither do I accuse you. Go and sin no more." Getting her to accept that statement for herself was often difficult.

ORGANIC DETERIORATION

The seventh step is organic deterioration.

In this final phase the alcoholic no longer cares how he looks. He is dirty and unshaven. His eyes are bleary, and his face is perpetually bloated and flushed.

A woman who reaches this level of alcohol addiction has the same lack of interest in her appearance. Her hair is disheveled, and her clothes are wrinkled. She may apply heavy layers of makeup to her pasty face in a futile effort to look as she once did, but she succeeds in deceiving no one, not even herself. Her interest in housekeeping is gone—dirty dishes pile up in the kitchen sink, papers are scattered over the living room furniture and the floor, cigarette butts fill the ashtrays and spill onto the carpet.

The alcoholic woman often sinks to prostitution or will take up with any man who will provide her with a place to stay and furnish her the alcohol she now requires. She hates herself for it but sees no other way out.

At this final stage the alcoholic is no longer a good worker. Previously he worked hard to cover up his bouts with alcohol. His constant drinking has cost him one job after another until he has reached the place where he no longer attempts to work at all. An occasional job is only a means of getting a few dollars for alcohol and room rent, and finally just for alcohol. By this time his mind is so befuddled he can't be used for anything requiring skill.

His health is about gone as well. The body God gave him has finally begun to break down under constant neglect and abuse. Anyone who has ever visited skid row has seen evidences of the deterioration that grips these victims in the final stages of alcohol addiction. They stumble haltingly along the street like men twice their age. Walking is torture, and their hands tremble. They eke out a miserable existence on handouts. Malnutrition is common, as are cirrhosis of the liver and nervous and gastric disorders. In France, where the rate of alcoholism is higher than anywhere else in the world, the incidence of liver ailments is the highest.

I can speak personally about the gastric disorders caused by alcoholism, because I burned up my stomach with alcohol during my drinking days.

The alcoholic may have circulatory problems and break out in "wine sores," as we called them at the mission. At this stage he is no stranger to hospitals. He has undoubtedly had the experience of collapsing and being taken to the charity ward in a hospital, where they have treated him as best they could. The medical profession finds working with such men or women a frustrating, fruitless task. Their bodies have been abused so terribly they do not respond well to treatment. And when they are discharged, they almost invariably go back to the bottle and continue the process of destroying themselves.

The family doctor of an acquaintance of mine tried hard to get him to quit drinking, but with no success. Finally, after being called out again in the middle of the night to stop him from hemorrhaging, he was exasperated.

"Ole," he exploded, "I've told you a hundred times that you're going to kill yourself if you keep this up. The next time you feel like drinking, will you do me a favor? Take a good strong dose of strychnine instead. The result will be the same, and it'll save us both a lot of trouble."

Ole continued to drink. Less than three months later he hemorrhaged again. This time the doctor was unable to stop it. He couldn't pour blood into Ole's worn-out body fast enough to do any good, and he bled to death.

Even more disturbing than an alcoholic's physical deterioration is the way his mind deteriorates. Every mission superintendent sees this effect of alcohol, even in former professional men—bankers, lawyers, investment brokers, and business executives.

The mind and personality of a former medical doctor, who finally died at a state institution, was so affected by his continual bouts with alcohol that he could not learn to live outside an institution. This man, who at one time had been a useful member of society and highly respected and loved in his community, could not even be used in a minor way as a male nurse at the institution where he spent the final years of his life. His once-fine mind had been virtually destroyed by his drinking.

A wealthy Kansas wheat farmer, whose net worth was judged at close to a million dollars, was so ruined by alcohol that ten years later his fortune was gone, and he was living on skid row. He washed dishes in a cheap café and barely did well enough to keep from losing his job.

While I was at the mission in Omaha a young man came in. He took pride in the fact that he had not gone as far down as some of those he saw around him.

"Listen, buster," I said to him, "don't get so smug about that. You're on the road. You aren't all the way down yet, but wait awhile. You'll get there."

I never saw him again, but I do know I told him the truth. Unless he got his life straightened out he would wind up exactly like the others he professed to despise.

The possibility of going all the way down faces any individual from the third stage down. And there is a possibility that it will happen to many of the social and habitual drinkers who haven't been drinking long enough to become addicts. Fortunately, however, no one has to reach the place of organic deterioration before being set free from the bondage of alcohol. At any place along the downward path he can face himself and his situation and throw off the shackles of addiction.

The sooner the individual makes the decision to quit drinking and seek help, the less hold beverage alcohol will have on him and the easier it will be for him to be freed. The man or woman in the final stage of alcoholism is not impossible to reach by any means, though, for nothing is impossible with God. But the problems involved become more grave the longer he waits to get help.

For example, we had a music professor from a large high school who had been an alcoholic only for a year and a half when he came for help. Working with him was much different from working with men who had been alcoholics for ten or fifteen years. He responded to treatment and suggestion much faster and didn't have the relapses that so often mark the alcoholic's path back to sobriety.

Unfortunately, nothing can be done for the alcoholic until he wants to be reached. You may recognize all the symptoms and know what the fellow needs, but you can't get through to him unless he wants help. In counseling I have reached the place through long and sometimes bitter experience where I will refuse to talk to a person who doesn't personally ask for help.

On one occasion a pastor urged me to visit a family in which the husband was an alcoholic. I tried to explain that my visit would be fruitless unless the husband wanted to be helped. But when the wife pleaded with me to see him, I agreed.

I spent half the morning getting acquainted with him and developing a measure of rapport. If I were to help him, I had to gain his confidence. Finally, he began to open up, and we were able to start a friendly discussion about his problem and the solution to it. Then his wife came into the room. As she listened, she was irritated by something he said. Immediately she broke into the conversation, tearing him apart in front of me. That ended any hope I had of reaching him. It was a miserable, embarrassing situation, and I soon excused myself and left.

The situation was hopeless from the start. The man wasn't ready for help and didn't want it. He hadn't contacted me, so he didn't really want to talk to me. When I went to his home I was an intruder. We didn't have the privacy we should have had. Furthermore, I hadn't had an opportunity to get acquainted with his wife, so I didn't know what to expect from her. When she tore into her husband I was helpless. I realize that all the past humiliation and heartaches and her present fears had probably brought her to the point where she could no longer contain herself. Nevertheless, my visit did nothing to help them and may have been a hindrance.

The alcoholic must reach a crisis point in his life before he will be open to guidance and help. He has to hit bottom. That bottom is different in each individual life.

One well-known attorney was a prealcoholic when he hit bottom. A fastidious dresser, well-mannered and dignified, he was just the opposite when he was intoxicated. His wife tried to tell him what a fool he made of himself when he had drunk too much, but he wouldn't believe it. So at a cocktail party she had a friend come in with a video camera and tape what he did. When he was sober they screened it for him.

He never took another drink.

Various surveys have estimated that only 3 to 12 percent of alcohol addicts ever get to skid row. The vast majority are living in their communities, protected by their families and occasionally by their business associates. They hide in their prisons of shame, fearful of facing life. Most do not even want to admit to themselves that they have a problem. They must be jolted by something that shocks them enough to cause them to hit bottom and begin to look for answers.

A man may hit bottom when he loses his job for the first time and sees his wife and family without any means of support. Perhaps he hits bottom when the children recognize the problem and speak about it.

One woman came to my office in desperation after such an experience. She had come home with a six-pack of beer. Her twelve-year-old son fell to his knees and grabbed her around the legs and cried, "Oh, Mommy, Mommy, please don't drink that stuff! You know what it does to you!"

What he said caused her to seek help.

Another woman came to me about her husband. "I have told that man a hundred times that I was going to leave him if he didn't quit drinking."

"Have you ever left him?" I asked her.

"No."

"Well, leave him this time."

When her husband came home and found her gone, he was so stunned he realized he had to have help. Up until that moment he had thought she was only threatening. He had never recognized the fact that he had a drinking problem. Now he knew that everything worth having would be gone unless he faced up to this problem and got some answers. Consequently, he began to look for ways out of his difficulty.

Those who counsel alcoholics have to look for this type of experience. Part 2 of this book will deal with ways to help the alcoholic come to the point where he will seek help.

FOUR
COMPLETING THE CYCLE

Working with alcoholics through the years, we were disturbed by a number of things we could not understand. We could see how men and women would start drinking socially and progress downward until they hit bottom and faced up to the fact that they had a drinking problem. We knew they had a sincere desire to quit. We were also aware that when they really wanted to quit, they were in a position where they could be helped.

We saw them go through the awful agony of withdrawal. We saw men who had lost their jobs or had seen their businesses fail. Their wives had filed for divorce, and the mortgages on their homes had been foreclosed. Some suffered the ignominy of having their children placed with foster parents. Those men wanted to stay sober more than anything else in the world. They wanted to get their families back and once more have a place of respectability in the community. Yet they went back to drinking. Why did they fail? What were the warning signals? Could anything be done to help them break the vicious circle in which they found themselves?

For years such questions perplexed us. Back when I was at the mission in Omaha a man came in one night who obviously needed medical attention. We took him to the hospital. When we got him to the door of the psychiatric ward he had a seizure. Several attendants were needed to put him in bed and hold him until the medication calmed him.

He was in a private room where he spent the terrifying days of withdrawal; seeing strange, frightening crawling things on the wall; dreaming terrible dreams; suffering torments that those who have not experienced them cannot possibly understand. At last medication and hospital care and a period of sobriety cleared away the hallucinations. The man's mind began to function, and the doctors released him from the hospital.

He had a sincere desire never to take another drink. Had he been a millionaire and able to buy sobriety for the rest of his life, he would have given his entire fortune to have it. He was intelligent and had a good future ahead of him. Only one obstacle blocked his path—alcohol. I was certain this man had plenty of reason to stay sober. Still, in a matter of months, he was once more hitting the bottle.

The same thing had happened in my own life. I don't know how many times I tried to overcome the problem. Repeatedly I told myself, "It's going to be different from now on. I'm not going to take another drink." But I wasn't any stronger than the man to whom I just referred. Time after time I went back to drinking.

In our years of working with alcoholics, we observed a cycle: the alcoholic decides to quit drinking; he goes into a period of abstinence; he returns to the bottle.

We asked God for wisdom and understanding, claiming the promise found in James 1:5: "If any of you lack wisdom, let him ask of God, who giveth to all men liberally, and upbraideth not; and it shall be given him." In answer to our prayer, God gave the insight that helped us piece the pattern together, and we used this insight in our interviews with men who professed a saving knowledge of Christ. We discovered that almost invariably they followed the same cycle.

We tested that theory with forty-five men in the rehabilitation program in Omaha. All of them had made so many decisions to quit drinking that they had long since lost count. They had all gone back, in agony, into the awful blackness of alcoholism.

Without exception they agreed that we were right. There was a cycle, easily predictable, that most alcoholics followed. In understanding the alcoholic, it will help to consider this cycle and how it operates.

Although the cycle follows the same general pattern each time it is repeated, the length of time required for a full circle varies widely. A cycle could take place in a single week, three weeks, that many months, or even a number of years. A medical doctor with whom we came in contact took ten years to complete the cycle, but complete it he did.

Similarly, the segments or compartments that make up the cycle don't take the same amount of time in each case. The individual's makeup, the life he previously lived, and his current environment all affect the pattern.

During the cycle we saw the alcoholic go through four stages: (1) the desire never to take another drink, (2) pride of sobriety, (3) fear of drinking again, and (4) the feeling that he has finally mastered the situation.

THE DESIRE NEVER TO TAKE ANOTHER DRINK

The alcoholic has "had it." He's never going through the horror of being controlled by alcohol again. He's never going to be as sick as he was this time. Nor will he go through the nightmare of an alcoholic blackout. Never again will he have to pick up the pieces after an episode of not knowing what he has done while drunk. Never again will he wake up in a strange town not knowing how he got there. Never again will he be in a place where he doesn't know anyone or have a single friend to whom he can turn. Never again will he experience the feelings of guilt and remorse that flood his heart when he starts to sober up.

No, never again.

Just remembering the past keeps him sober for a time, and things go fairly well.

A woman in a small Nebraska town was like that. Her daughter would come, periodically, to a recovered alcoholic friend of ours, exulting in the way her alcoholic mother was doing.

"I just came from the house," she said, "and Mom is still sober. She had fixed herself up, and the house was clean. I know she's going to make it this time."

THE PRIDE OF SOBRIETY

The same woman shared her daughter's pride in the fact that she had gone several months without drinking. It had been some time since she had any tremors in her stomach. The cobwebs began to leave her mind, and she was feeling more like herself.

The Bible warns us not to think of ourselves more highly than we ought to think. It also tells us that we should take heed when we think we stand, lest we fall. Pride is dangerous.

When I was actively engaged in rescue mission work, men often came in proud of their accomplishment in leaving liquor alone. "I haven't had a drink in three weeks."

Another would say, "I haven't had a drink in a month, and I want you to know that I'm proud of it. I'm so thankful that I don't take that stuff anymore."

It isn't long until they have a superior attitude when they see others around them who are still drinking. "Did you see the way that guy acted?" they would say. "I'd never do anything like that—and in front of such nice people."

The recovering alcoholic soon forgets that he used to act the same way. He swells with pride because he is sure the situation is under control. He doesn't drink anymore!

Such thinking often coincides with the time the alcoholic starts to work again and is just beginning to produce. He has earned a little money, has bought himself some new clothes, and is beginning to enjoy the feel of having a few dollars in his pocket. He has returned to his home and his wife and children. His children are beginning to trust him, and his wife is beginning to treat him as a human being. As far as he is concerned, everything is going along just fine.

He's never been happier. The first thing he does when he sees you is tell you about the progress he has made and that he's getting back to the old feel of things. Pride of attainment shows in his facial expressions, his speech, and actions. What's more, he is convinced that he is once more in control of his life. But something is gnawing at him— something he probably doesn't mention to anyone.

THE FEAR OF DRINKING AGAIN

Even though the alcoholic longs to remain an abstainer, he has the urge to drink. A Christian woman in North Platte, Nebraska, was working with a woman alcoholic. She had managed to remain sober but had reached this point in the circle.

"Ethel," she confided to her counselor one day, "I'm terrified when I think of you and Gib going on vacation next month. I'm afraid I'll start to drink again when I don't have you to talk to."

In attempting to understand her, we must not forget that she is trying to make a comeback in a society that embraces social drinking with both arms. In most strata of society it is the accepted thing.

The alcoholic feels that he has to have a little social life, and common sense tells him that there are certain meetings and parties he has to attend in connection with his job. Many of those meetings will provide opportunities for drinking. It is difficult to go anywhere without having someone offer him a drink.

He's still proud of his attainment—he hasn't succumbed to the temptation to drink. He can still remember what it was like when he was hitting the bottle heavily. He realizes there is a chance he might lose all he has gained. The fear that he is going to take another drink begins to build.

This is the area we call a "dry drunk." The individual has reached the place where he has to fight against taking another drink. He is disgusted with those who drink. He can't stand the smell of liquor. He becomes irritable, and even the suggestion that he take a drink becomes a personal insult.

At the same time he begins to fight every beer sign that's hanging along the street, every ad he sees in the newspaper or on television. He wages a continual fight to keep from drinking and retain his hold on the life he now has.

I will never forget a terse note a respected business executive wrote me. "Jerry, this is still no picnic. Thanks to you, I know the scrap I have facing me. I surely hope the Lord intends for me to make the grade." There was a tone of hopelessness in his letter, a feeling that he was alone in his desperate battle to keep from taking another drink.

It would be easy to pity the man at this point, but pity can be devastating to the alcoholic's chances of attaining release. Pity can weaken his determination to fight the urge to drink and lead him to the conclusion that it's no use trying to remain sober.

The pressure against the individual who is fighting alcohol addiction is tremendous. Society encourages him to drink in many ways. The person who does not drink is looked upon as an oddball. The advertising media, movies, and television all promote and display a world where alcohol is freely consumed.

Yet the same society condemns a man if he lets his consumption of liquor get out of control. Just as pity is a hindrance to helping the alcoholic, so is condemnation.

And as the fight to keep from drinking increases, something else happens. Since he has not been drinking, his mind is clearer. He can think better, and the physical effects of excessive drinking are beginning to disappear. He is more and more like the normal, respectable person he used to be.

Combined with the pride that he hasn't taken a drink

for quite a while is the feeling that he has reached the place where he's finally going to be able to manage his life once more. He's really a different person from the one who had the drinking problem.

But at this point he may again become affected by the mental problem, personality quirk, or neurosis that caused him to drink in the first place. Dr. Clyde Narramore, in his pamphlet *Alcoholism*, suggests several possible reasons for that. The individual may be trying to hide from life. He may have reverted to alcoholism because of pressures and disturbances beyond his control. Those problems may still exist.

Dr. Narramore also calls attention to some physiological reasons for alcohol addiction:

> For example, the possibility of becoming an alcoholic is greater in persons who have undergone a condition known as anoxia at birth. This means that there was insufficient oxygen available for the body tissues. Also, it is known that certain neurological impairments can increase the probability of an individual becoming captured by drink. A complete physical examination should always be made while determining the cause of alcoholic addiction.

The alcoholic who is struggling to make a recovery and is fighting his burning desire to drink may also have some psychological, physical, or spiritual problem to add to his difficulties.

As he is beginning to recover, he is also saying to himself, "I'm feeling better physically and mentally than I ever have."

Somehow he believes that he has overcome the problems that caused him to drink or that aggravated his situation. He may feel that he's all right spiritually if he has started attending church again, even if he has never had a personal experience with Christ.

In spite of the battle he is having with his old desires to drink, he feels good. Because of that he thinks that everything is finally all right.

The Conviction That It Has Been Mastered

The recovering alcoholic begins to think that he can handle this thing. At last he has it under control.

The Scriptures warn us that pride always goes before a fall. Peter was sure that he would die with Christ rather than deny Him. But later, when he was asked if he also was a follower of Christ, he cursed and said he didn't even know Him. The alcoholic who is so sure he has finally mastered his problem is like Peter in his self-confidence.

It must be remembered that the alcoholic still lives in the world of social drinking. Ever since he first started a comeback, he has been pressured to drink by people who can't stand to see someone with more courage and will-power and good judgment than themselves.

They used to try their tactics on me. "You can handle it. What's the matter with you? Are you a man or a mouse? You're bigger than one little drink."

Just saying no doesn't stop them.

The fire chief in a small town fought his way to sobriety and for more than twenty years was dry. Then someone decided to have a beer party for the fire department, and friends taunted him into drinking again.

"Just one beer," they told him.

He died five years later of physical problems aggravated by his return to alcoholism. Those last years of his life were a torment to him because he could no longer stay sober.

Often, however, those who are still dry don't realize that their reason for not drinking has changed. They used to be proud of the fact that they no longer drank. Now the only reason they don't drink is because they are fighting it. They are scared to death that they are going to break down and have another drink. And they know that if that happens they will be in trouble again. Yet the stages are so subtle, the alcoholic may not realize what is happening without stopping and examining his motives.

THE FINAL STEP

Things have been going so well for the alcoholic that he has become complacent about his problem of alcohol addiction. He has been given more responsibility at work and quite possibly has had a raise or two. His wife is trusting him more than she has for some time. His children have more confidence in him, and that increases his confidence in himself. He's the master of a whole new world. He is now back to the place where he was when he first began to drink socially—or so he thinks. When he is urged to take a drink, he does so, thinking that by now he surely ought to be able to handle it.

What happens after that doesn't follow a set pattern. If he has taken one drink and was able to stop before he got drunk he is more proud of himself than ever. He believes he can again drink socially and handle it. His guard goes down, and he loses some of his fear of alcohol.

Or one drink might set the fires of alcoholism raging out of control in his life. One drink can create an insatiable thirst that will not be quenched. One drink might be enough to plunge him to the very depths of alcoholism as quickly as one can be pushed over a cliff.

The alcoholic who takes another drink—whether he takes the slow or the fast route—will experience the same result: He will once again be completely victimized by alcohol addiction.

One fellow I had been working with had me stumped. I knew him well but couldn't figure out what was building the fire that caused him to turn back to the bottle periodically. Everything seemed to be going well for him. His wife was a lovely Christian, and he had been taken in by her friends and their husbands in a wonderful way; so he wasn't with people who would encourage him to drink. Yet he had started drinking again.

One day I was talking with his wife when the answer came. "Joe likes the taste of beer, so he drinks near beer. He figures there's no harm in that since there's no alcohol in it."

There isn't much ethyl alcohol in near beer, but there is a little—one half of 1 percent. That doesn't sound like much, but for some reason the trace of ethyl alcohol in near beer was enough to start him drinking again. He had reached the place in alcoholism that diabetics reach when they have no tolerance for sugar. Ethyl alcohol triggers such fierce thirst and craving in the alcoholic that he inevitably goes back into drunkenness.

Earlier in this chapter we mentioned a doctor who had a ten-year cycle. By drinking half a glass of beer, he started on another drunk that brought him the ruination of his home and cost him his practice. Previously an alcoholic, he had fought his way up through the cycle. He had won back his practice and was building a good life for himself.

His friends drank, however, and since he felt he should serve them liquor when he entertained, he kept a supply on hand. For some reason, those who drink do not feel comfortable being around someone who isn't drinking with the others. In order to make his guests feel comfortable he always poured himself half a glass of beer and set it in front of him, never touching it.

He married a second time and went out to San Francisco for a reunion of his old navy buddies, taking his bride along. As usual, he poured half a glass of beer and set it in front of him. While everybody was spinning yarns about the old days, he reached out and drank the half glass of beer. Months later he stumbled into the mission in Omaha where he told me that he had downed that beer before he even realized what he was doing. Although he had been dry for ten years, that half glass of beer was enough to pull the trigger.

When he reaches this stage in the cycle of chronic alcoholism, the individual's body once again begins to deteriorate. The same situations happen to him, the same DTs terrify him, the same despair grips his soul like an ugly recurring nightmare, until he once more reaches the place where he can't take it any longer. And again he decides he never wants another drink.

He has come back to the place he began, and, unhappily, the cycle will repeat and keep repeating until some way is found to break it.

It is when the alcoholic is at the bottom—the place where he doesn't ever want to take another drink—that we can help him break the cycle. This is only possible because God has provided a way of escape. This will be developed fully in part 2, but we will consider here briefly some of the things you can do to help:

1. Encourage the alcoholic in his desire to stop drinking.
2. Help him face his problem.
3. Provide him with the medical care that he needs. See that he gets a complete physical checkup.
4. Help him understand that he can't overcome alcohol addiction by himself.
5. Introduce him to the power of God.
6. Teach him to keep in daily touch with God's power.

These are the ways we will be able to help the alcoholic break the cycle and overcome addiction. It is possible for him to be completely free from the power of alcohol addiction.

These are the goals we must aim for and encourage the alcoholic to strive for. Being sober isn't enough. He can only come to the place of real victory over every phase of his life through faith in the Lord Jesus Christ. That faith will give him victory over drinking now and a place with God in all eternity.

One thing that impressed me when I was at the mission, whether in talking with one of the men from the street or with an "up and out" alcoholic, was that every case is different. And the approach to the problem must be slightly different with every individual because God has not made us all the same.

For that reason there is no standard procedure; there

are no hard and fast rules that can be followed in every case. Yet God is vitally interested in every man. God is willing to give us the wisdom and insight needed in every case if we will only look to Him and not to man for the answers.

That does not mean we should not use psychiatrists or doctors or sociologists. God gives us capable men in those professions to help with such problems. But we must not lose sight of the fact that in the last analysis God is the One who heals.

FIVE

THE FAMILY OF THE ALCOHOLIC— HINDRANCE AND HELP

Dr. Stephen A. Seymour, who operated the Stephen A. Seymour Hospital for Alcoholics in Los Angeles, used to write a column for the Wilshire Press. In one of his columns he was asked a question.

> Dear Doctor:
> What gives you the greatest problem in the treatment of difficult case histories? Is it delirium tremens, malnutrition, vitamin deficiency, or temporary insanity?
> Joan H.

Dr. Seymour replied:

> Dear Joan H.:
> The biggest problem is in treating the members of the patient's family who don't drink.

How true that is!

At the mission we discovered that one of our greatest problems in helping a man back to usefulness was in dealing with his family.

THE ALIENATION OF THE FAMILY

For varying lengths of time the alcoholic had hurt everyone around him. That was particularly true of those who loved him the most. He had lied to them, abused them, and made them suffer in a way that few who have not been close to such an individual can understand.

Not long ago I was talking with a man whose wife had died of acute alcoholism. "You can't imagine what I went through," he said. "I got to the place where I thought I was the one who was losing my mind."

The hurt the alcoholic brings to his family is not necessarily intentional. In his progression into alcoholism he has experienced a complete breakdown of his own personality. Whatever he was before, he is now a selfish, self-centered individual. He has a burning desire for alcohol and wants to destroy anything that he thinks stands in the way of securing it. Often, in his warped state of mind, he thinks his family is the chief obstacle.

That was the way it was with me. My heart still aches as I recall sitting in my living room and looking at my own family (my wife and three children) with a strange, unnatural loathing. I had a good job. I was respected in the community. Yet my craving for alcohol burned so fiercely it was the only thing that mattered. It meant more than family or job or friends.

They weren't going to continue to stand in my way, I reasoned. I wasn't going to allow them to hold me down. I'd leave. Then I could drink all I wanted to without having them on my back trying to make me feel guilty for what I was doing.

My family had never given me any reason for feeling as I did. Most alcoholics, if they were completely honest, would have to admit the same thing. They hadn't nagged at me or tried to interfere with my life. Their only fault was that they were standing between me and my beloved bottle. I couldn't take it!

So I left home and went on a two-year drunk that lasted until a drastic situation stopped me from drinking.

Leaving my family was despicable, but at the time I had convinced myself that I was the innocent party who was being abused at every turn. I believed that I had been deeply hurt by my family. I had finally reached the place where I couldn't take the abuse any longer and got out. No one, I told myself, could blame me. There was just so much that a man could take.

During that period I gave little thought to what my actions had done to my family. Our oldest son had been hurt so deeply he was openly resentful. Our daughter was bewildered at having her father leave, and, because her mother had to work to support the family, she was placed in an orphanage. Our other son was too young to understand what was happening. Still, he sensed the confusion and unhappiness that swirled about him, and it blighted his life. My wife loved me and stayed by me through everything that had happened, yet I deserted her. It was a terrifying, traumatic experience for all of them.

When I finally came back home, although I had found Christ as my Savior and was determined to live for Him, they had a great adjustment to make. It wasn't easy to accept the fact that I had returned and wanted to make amends for the hurt and grief I had caused them. It was hard for them to believe that I wouldn't do the same thing again.

I didn't realize the full extent of what I had done and how it had affected my family until some years later when we visited our oldest son and his family in Denver. One morning he bared his heart to me as the two of us went for a drive.

"Your prayers must be paying off, Dad," he said suddenly. "I quit hating your guts three months ago."

He had done a good job of keeping me from knowing his true feelings. When we were there he was nice to me, and when we phoned them occasionally he was cordial; but beneath that veneer lay an ugly, open wound. He loved me during that period. If he hadn't he would have written me off long ago. But he was afraid I would fail, and he couldn't stand the thought of being hurt so deeply again.

My wife Greta's reaction was different. Although she had drifted far from God, she knew Christ as her Savior.

She realized that God was still sovereign and that somehow He would work things out. She had some serious adjustments to make, but through God's love she was able to overcome the hurt and accept me back into our home.

Our two younger children had little difficulty in accepting me. They saw me in the newness of the life of Christ, and His love warmed their hearts and took away their hurt.

Although we had problems and difficulties in making adjustments, some of the families we have tried to help have had considerably more trouble than we did.

The Family Can Hinder Recovery

Often the inclination of the alcoholic's family is either to pity him or reject him. Neither will do him any good. What he needs is intelligent understanding.

A wife will often become overly sympathetic when she is trying to win her husband away from alcohol. Because of that she will do things that will actually be a hindrance to him.

Take the distraught wife who called me one holiday season. Her husband had been drinking and was involved in an automobile accident. No one had been hurt, but because he was drunk, he was jailed. She wanted me to see about getting him released.

I had had some contact with him previously. He was concerned about his drinking and was looking for help. Thinking this might be the time that I could help him spiritually, I made arrangements with a bondsman and secured his release.

The next thing I knew, the man had lost his job and was on a real drunk. But that wasn't the end. Some time later I was called when things were in a worse mess than before. The family was out of money and hungry. The husband was in that terrible, bitter, accusing state of the alcoholic who hates everybody and everything that stands in the way of his drinking. When I got to their home I asked him how he got in the shape he was in.

"When you were in jail you had time to get the liquor out of your system, and you could have gone back to work the next day. What started this binge?"

He didn't answer, but his wife did, and what she said stunned me.

"I knew he'd be so shaky and feel so terrible after being in jail and being taken off liquor so suddenly," she told me. "So on the way home I stopped and got him a six-pack of beer and a pint of whiskey."

I didn't say a word. I couldn't. I got up and left.

Another woman wanted her husband to go to Alcoholics Anonymous. "I'll make a bargain with you," he said. "I'll go to AA if you'll give me a half-pint of whisky every time I go."

She was so anxious to have him start attending the AA meetings that she entered into the agreement. After he had gone to a number of meetings, she realized he wasn't being helped. The half-pint of whisky was spoiling anything the organization could do for him.

Regardless of how well-meaning, such sympathy for the alcoholic can only hinder any attempt he makes to quit drinking.

Bitterness and rejection can be just as harmful as pity. Although the spouse and family of every alcoholic suffers unspeakably, they must forgive and forget if they want to see this husband and father restored as a respected member of their family and of society.

Forgiving is never easy, and it is particularly difficult when the spouse runs the risk of being hurt again. It is so hard that only by a complete surrender to Christ can a spouse take back her erring mate without reservation.

There are many ways in which an alcoholic's mate can be a hindrance. One church brought to our attention the needs of a family with eight children. The father was an alcoholic, and often there wasn't food enough in the house. The church was able to meet some of the physical needs, but they asked me to try to help in the rehabilitation of the father.

During the period we were counseling him, the man stopped drinking from time to time, but he always went back to the bottle.

It was difficult to understand why. He was a fine musician and had played and sung with country-music bands from coast to coast. He would probably have stayed with this vocation had he not had such a large family. They were a hindrance.

"I'd like to go back to music," he would tell me wistfully. He spoke of it so often I began to see that part of his drinking problem was his feeling that he had failed his family. By staying with a band he could have earned enough money to support his family. That was a second hindrance.

Then one day the rest of the puzzle fell into place. I was visiting him one afternoon when I noticed that his wife wasn't there.

"She's at work and I'm baby-sitting," he blurted out miserably. "I'd like to get a job, but she doesn't want me to. I'm supposed to baby-sit." His eyes met mine. "And that's not being a man! I've got to be a man!"

But his wife had seen the time when her children had gone hungry because he failed them. Now she had a job and knew that she wouldn't lose it because of drinking. Her normal instinct to provide for her children was also destroying what she wanted most out of life—a husband and father who would provide for her and the children.

Some of the case histories I have compiled in my years of working with alcoholics provide insight into the reasons some men cannot quit drinking.

One man wrote, "I'm not trying to blame anyone. I only want to show what could be one of the reasons for my excessive drinking. In twenty-five years of marriage my wife has never once told me she loved me. By nature I am a very affectionate person, and I have constantly showed my love toward my wife and daughter. Never once has my wife returned any of my love. After we were separated for four years she informed me that her mind controlled her emotions."

For lack of love he began to do more and more drinking until he became a chronic alcoholic. The inability of one's life partner to return affection may keep the alcoholic drinking.

Another underlying difficulty for recovering alcoholics is a lack of cleanliness in the home. If the wife is a poor housekeeper, the house is always dirty and cluttered, the kids' faces need scrubbing and their clothes need washing and mending, it can provide a source of strife and an area of real difficulty for the counselor trying to help the alcoholic husband back to sobriety.

It may be that the wife is overworked or so distraught she has let the housework slide. Whatever the reason, the dirt and physical confusion of the home can add to the mental disruption of the alcoholic and make it more difficult for him to keep off alcohol.

Let's take a look at the situation from the alcoholic's point of view. He knows he has messed up his life, but he is more anxious than ever to get his family back. Now that he's put the bottle aside, he is going to clean up his life. He comes back home eager for things to be different.

But when he gets there, home is the same as it was when he left. The sink is stacked with dirty dishes, and the stove hasn't been cleaned for a year. Newspapers are strewn all over the floor. The dirt under the bed has been there for six months. It's the same dirty old hole. His wife's habits haven't changed. He was foolish to think that they would, or that he could change.

I am not sure I understand why a dirty house should be a hindrance to a man who is trying to shake alcohol addiction, but it is. To have success with an alcoholic who is married to a poor housekeeper, the counselor must make her see the importance of a clean, attractive home.

Just as some wives are careless about the home and the care of the children, some husbands are careless about their finances. This can cause many serious problems, especially for the wife who drinks socially.

If the husband is irresponsible in caring for the needs

of his family and is extravagant and irresponsible, financial trouble sets in. Bill collectors start to hound them. The bank calls, telling them their checking account is overdrawn. The wife is humiliated, angry, and worried. If she is a social drinker, she may begin to drink more to hide from her problems, and in a matter of time may become an alcoholic.

If such a woman is to be helped, her husband must be helped to handle his financial matters in order to remove the pressures that have been causing his wife to drink.

One woman, distressed by her husband's excessive drinking, decided to start drinking herself. She had the warped idea that somehow her drinking would cause him to quit. Then she would quit, and they would both be dry. But that wasn't the way it worked out. She became an alcoholic as well, and the two of them lived miserable lives before a faithful Christian began to deal with them. Another hindrance is the guilt complex that enshrouds the family of the alcoholic man or woman. The nondrinking or social-drinking members of the family are terribly ashamed. They are ashamed of the way the alcoholic has acted in the neighborhood or in front of guests in the home. They find it difficult to accept the fact that their loved one is addicted. Often they will not seek outside help until the situation becomes so serious they are desperate.

Not long ago a businessman called me in desperation and wanted to know what could be done to help his wife. "She's an alcoholic," he said. "I finally had to do something with her, so I put her in the hospital; but she's as bad off now as when she went in."

The rest of the story was equally discouraging. The doctors recommended that she be sent to a sanatorium for a year at a cost of $18,000. "I can afford that for a little while," he said, "but not for long."

This couple belonged to the country club set. Among their friends, drinking was the accepted method of entertaining. Both of them drank socially, but the wife was more susceptible to alcohol than her husband. She attended cocktail parties and bridge clubs where she consumed more and more liquor. Her desire to be popular, to be socially acceptable, and to be included in the activities of society became a stumbling block and sent her into alcoholism. Now she was to be hospitalized for a year or more at great expense.

Social drinking itself presents a problem when the alcoholic is trying to make a proper adjustment to his family.

A friend of mine had been sober for more than sixteen years when he came to my office to talk to me. "My wife has gone back to social drinking," he said. "She likes a glass of beer on a warm summer day. I can't see anything much wrong with that, so I buy it for her."

He didn't realize the danger of his susceptibility to the alcoholic cycle. The very fact that his wife was drinking could start him fighting alcohol and throw him into the dry drunk stage. He would see her enjoying a drink and know there was more in the refrigerator. All he would have to do would be to go out and take one. One of those days he could become tired of fighting his desire for a glass of beer, and, unless he had given himself completely over to the Lord, he might not be strong enough spiritually to resist. The first time he opened a can of beer and drank it, he would be in big trouble.

A similar and perhaps even more serious problem exists for the alcoholic woman whose husband drinks socially. He may have liquor in the house with the understanding that she is not to drink it. But if she does not work and remains home all day, she has liquor readily available and no one to persuade her not to drink. The chances for making a comeback under circumstances like that are very, very small. But a right relationship with God and a good solid grounding in the Christian faith can assure any alcoholic of overcoming the difficulties of readjusting to his family.

When I started in the field of alcohol therapy, little was done for the family. Most of the attention was focused on the alcoholic—he was the one with the problem. Today it is common to hear the term "co-alcoholic" in seminars on alcoholism. It is a move in the right direction. The entire family is adversely affected by the alcoholic loved one. The drinking of a member of the family leaves them all emotionally and psychologically scarred. It can even leave family members with physical problems. They need attention and treatment as well. Alcoholism is truly a family disease.

The family of an alcoholic is robbed. Life has literally been taken away from them—emotionally, physically, spiritually, socially, and vocationally. The family of the alcoholic moves in society as a hurt and broken unit, desperately seeking a ray of hope in what seems to them a hopeless situation.

Children are probably the worst sufferers. They have been abused—many times unintentionally—by mothers or fathers so drunk they were not aware of their actions. When I was in Lincoln we saw many children at our family shelter who were black and blue or had broken ribs or arms.

Claire C. Costales, in her book *The Way Back to Reality* tells of a six-year-old girl whose father came in to kiss her goodnight. He was drunk and passed out as he bent over her, falling across her small body. She was almost smothered to death before the mother was able to move him. That girl, though she is grown now, still has a great sense of fear whenever her father comes near her.

Fear rules the family of the average alcoholic. There is even a fear of calling for help, particularly if the alcoholic is working—as 85 to 90 percent are. The spouse is afraid to call for help for fear the alcoholic will lose his job and the family income will be gone.

Then there is the fear of the community, the fear of being labeled as that family with an alcoholic husband or wife. The family will often put up with drunken rages and physical abuse in an effort to keep their neighbors from knowing their true situation. Often there is as much denial of the problem by the family as there is by the alcoholic. Strangely enough, they probably aren't really keeping a secret. Neighbors, friends, and acquaintances are usually already aware that a family member has a serious drinking problem.

Then there is the fear of having the true cause of the problem known in the community. Every problem has two sides. Often, the family of the alcoholic doesn't want their part in the difficulty to become public knowledge.

I have seen a number of women who have been mistreated by an alcoholic husband finally to go through a divorce only to marry another problem drinker. It didn't make sense to me until I discovered that many of those were domineering women. They wanted to have their own way with their children and in the operation of their homes. They didn't want to share the authority with anyone. They could not submit themselves to the authority of their husbands, and their attitude had a tendency to destroy their mates. In such circumstances men will often resort to drink and destroy themselves with alcohol, which makes it easier for their wives to take over the authority of the home.

I have also seen women put up with abuse from their alcoholic spouses for years, praying that they would be set free from alcohol and live a new, productive life. If her prayers are answered, however, the wife sometimes cannot cope with a sober, conscientious husband and divorces him.

In *Rx for Addiction*, by W. Robert Gehring, Dr. Gehring's wife, Carolyn, relates the difficulty she had in relinquishing the reins to their finances and control of the home and the children after her husband's conversion and return to a normal alcohol- and drug-free life. She was able to make the adjustment only after a long and bitter struggle with herself.

A judge in Oregon lived a life of debauchery and drunkenness for twenty years before he confessed his sin and received Christ as his Savior. His wife, who had half the church praying for his salvation, left him and took up with another wastrel. It was several years later when she was desperately in fear of her life that she called the judge and asked him to help her. Today they have re-married and are very happy. But she is one of the unusual ones. Many domineering women seem to prefer having their own way, even if it means beatings, abuse, and sometimes poverty.

So the family of the alcoholic is often a very sick family. Earlier we quoted a man with an alcoholic wife as saying, "I got to the point where I thought I was crazy." He is far from alone in that feeling of frustration and bewilderment. It is important for the church to recognize the problems of the family members of an alcoholic and work for their successful recovery. God's love can change the family as well as the alcoholic.

THE FAMILY NEEDS HELP

The spouse of the alcoholic must also reach the place where he or she is willing to ask for help. We must encourage them to let their alcoholic loved ones know that they are going to seek help. We need to help them reach the place where they are willing to explain to their alcoholics the value of going to the family meetings of Alcoholics Victorious or AA or to Al-Anon.

It is best to explain that the alcoholic may not take the news passively. He may fly into a rage or profess to be indifferent to it. But if the family of the alcoholic is going to recover, they must not react violently themselves or get defensive. Recovery can only come when they take their stand and live their lives without being judgmental or nagging.

I usually advise the wife to say something like this: "Honey, I need help and I'm going to get it. If I get help, and you reach the place where you want help, I'll be able to help you."

The alcoholic's family must also make sure that the money supply is protected—that they are not in the position where everything they have can be spent for liquor. It is quite possible that legal assistance will be needed to accomplish that. Sometimes the personnel department of the company the husband works for can help.

The wife should not be afraid to approach her husband's employer. Most employers would like to help the alcoholic make a successful recovery. Many times the alcoholic has worked for the same company for twenty years or more. It costs far less to help an alcoholic recover than it does to fire him and train someone else to take his job. If the alcoholic is able to stop drinking, his absenteeism will go down and production will go up. He won't make as many errors, and, if he is in a position of authority, his decisions will be more sound. In short, he will be a better worker and make more money for the firm.

Many companies have employee assistance programs that are designed to help the worker with drinking problems. The personnel director can inform the wife if any such program exists in their company. He also would be likely to know about the assistance that may be available on a community-wide basis.

The families of alcoholics have been browbeaten and put down for years. They have isolated themselves from their friends, their churches, and the social activities they would normally be attending. They need to develop a social life, taking part in the things that go on at the church even if their alcoholic loved one will not attend. They need to be encouraged to stand and help the alcoholic without fear. They must show him that they will not allow him to dominate their lives.

At the family shelter in Lincoln we tried to get the families of alcoholics involved in the therapy program so we could discuss their problems with them. If it was possible we got every member of the family in those sessions so they would be able to understand the problem and the part they would be able to play in the successful recovery.

THE FAMILY CAN HELP RECOVERY

It is imperative that the sober spouse establish a family routine of meals and bedtimes and other activities. Once that routine is established it must be kept. It helps to give the children, who by this time inevitably feel insecure and unloved, a feeling of trust and a secure atmosphere. But it is not only the children who are helped by regular habits. Every member of the family can draw strength from them.

It is also important that the family members become accountable to each other. They must learn to be open with each other. That doesn't come without work and conscious effort, but it does provide encouragement for one another. The family members learn to look at things together; to see that what they do affects the others in the family. It helps to provide a sense of unity when their home life has been all but shattered.

There must be a display of love within the family, especially during the time of recovery. Children must know that they are loved in spite of the problems that seem sure to destroy them. They have to see that there is a solid, loving attitude that will not allow decay to set in.

Family members must be honest with one another, always. That can help to build trust and love as few things can.

It is obvious that the changes that are necessary in the life of the family for recovery are not going to happen immediately. No magic wand exists to wave every act into its rightful place and to restore immediately what took months or years to destroy. The wife, husband and children must be brought together and the problems worked out through the efforts of the entire family. It is a learning experience, and there will be many failures.

Shortly after the first edition of *God Is for the Alcoholic* came out a doctor in Omaha referred a woman to me. He had given her a copy of the book, and though she hadn't read it, it interested her.

Her alcoholic husband had left her, and she was hurt, bitter, and emotionally ill. I felt led to share my experience with her. I told her how I left my wife. Greta hadn't known where I was for two years, and when she did find me I was on my way to spend two years in the Texas prison system.

When I returned to my family, it hadn't been easy for Greta to take me back. She did so in spite of her fear that I would start drinking and leave her again. I hadn't realized how difficult it was for her until I came home one afternoon from making hospital calls. I was in the first year of a pastorate, and it had been six years since I started on the road to recovery.

As I walked into the kitchen she looked up and said, "Honey, this afternoon I made up my mind that you're going to make it."

Several days later the woman I had been counseling phoned. "Everything is going to be all right," she said.

"Has your husband come back?"

"No, but I've read your book, and I know where I have to change so when he does come back everything will be all right."

I still do not know whether her husband came back, but I do know she had learned an important lesson—not to be a stumbling block for her alcoholic husband when he did return.

The family will heal much faster and more surely if they spend time as a family around God's Word. The true foundation for happiness must be introduced for the family to be transformed. Jesus Christ in the hearts of the members of the family will change the lives of each one and make victory over alcohol and the accompanying sins and hurts a certainty.

SIX

WHAT GOD SAYS

WHAT DOES THE BIBLE SAY?

Every now and then a fellow used to come staggering into my office at the Open Door Mission, shake a finger in my face, and slur a challenge at me that he was certain would shut me up for all time.

"Jerry!" His voice mushed the words. "It's all right for me to drink. The Bible says so! I dare you to show me anywhere in the Bible where it says that I can't drink!"

One time a woman who was obviously drunk phoned me. "I know I drink," she announced defiantly, "but I've been saved, and I know I'm saved. If I was so stinkin' drunk I fell in the gutter and died, I know I'd go to heaven!"

What can we say to people like that? And what scriptural basis can we have for what we do say?

For years that was a big problem for me. Back in 1948 when I accepted the Lord Jesus Christ as my Savior I simply took Him at His Word. Some of the Scripture verses I rested on were: "For whosoever shall call upon the name of the Lord shall be saved" (Romans 10:13).

"He that heareth my word, and believeth on him that sent me, hath everlasting life, and shall not come into condemnation; but is passed from death unto life" (John 5:24).

"But as many as received him, to them gave he power to become the sons of God, even to them that believe on his name" (John 1:12).

"For by grace are ye saved through faith; and that not of yourselves: it is the gift of God: not of works, lest any man should boast" (Ephesians 2:8-9).

"So then faith cometh by hearing, and hearing by the word of God" (Romans 10:17).

I was convinced in my heart and mind of the truth of the Scriptures, and I had found Christ as my Savior. I knew I had been given a new life, for the Bible said so: "Therefore if any man be in Christ, he is a new creature: old things are passed away; behold, all things are become new" (2 Corinthians 5:17).

Then I began to hear temperance lectures in which the speakers went to great lengths to explain that there were two Hebrew words, *yayin* and *tirosh*, and two Greek words, *oinos* and *gleukos*, which were translated as "wine" in English. Yet, so the speakers declared, one word in each language meant unfermented wine and the other referred to fermented wine.

I searched the Scriptures and read what authorities had to say on the subject, but could find no place where the statements concerning different meanings of the two words were borne out. Dr. Roland H. Bazinon, professor of Ecclesiastical History at Yale University, wrote in *Christianity Today* (7 July 1958) that all four words refer to fermented wine, and he quoted portions of the Bible to prove it.

The interpretation of the temperance people bothered me a great deal. I believe the Bible is the Word of God. I believe it says what it means and means what it says and that it needs no other interpreter. I base my salvation upon it—my hope for eternal life.

When I tell a man that he is born again and has new life because the Word of God says so, I believe it with all my heart. I believe that he can trust the promises of God and can take the Bible for exactly what it says.

Consider the man who was trying to trap me with his argument from the Bible. Suppose I had tried to explain away the word *wine* in the Bible. Suppose I told him that it doesn't really mean wine, even though it says wine. Later, when I tried to talk with him about his soul I would use a verse like Romans 10:9-10: "That if thou shalt confess with thy mouth the Lord Jesus, and shalt believe in thine heart that God hath raised him from the dead, thou shalt be saved. For with the heart man believeth unto righteousness; and with the mouth confession is made unto salvation."

If he should make a decision for Christ, and I told him that now he could know he was saved he might question me. "When I was talking to you about wine you said the Bible doesn't really mean wine. Now you say the Bible says that I'm saved. How can I believe you? Maybe it means something else when it says that I'm saved."

That is hypothetical, but with the men who frequent a rescue mission that is exactly what would have happened. I couldn't use any argument with them that wasn't scriptural. In searching the Bible, I wasn't able to find anything it said against drinking, but the Word of God does have a lot to say against drunkenness. One of the more familiar portions is Proverbs 20:1: "Wine is a mocker, strong drink is raging: and whosoever is deceived thereby is not wise."

The Bible does not say anything about not drinking wine, except to several different classes of people. When wine was used in the prescribed way according to God's plan and purpose, He accepted it. But when man's misuse resulted in drunkenness, God condemned it.

So when I was challenged to show someone where the Bible says he shouldn't drink (and this used to happen often), I had an answer. "Friend of mine," I would say, "the Bible doesn't say that you shouldn't drink."

They usually blinked at that. It was entirely unexpected.

"There isn't any place in the Bible that says you shouldn't drink. But it does have a lot to say about getting drunk. Let me give you a few examples." Then I would read some Bible verses along that line. From there I would proceed to show him in the Word that he was a sinner, that he needed a Savior because he had committed sins against the holy God.

Invariably that would throw the person off guard. Instead of an argument, which is what he expected, he had been brought face to face with his sin and the provision God has made through Christ to forgive him and make him a new creature.

Read Jeremiah 13:9-14, and you will see that God uses alcohol as a judgment. And later in the same book you read: "Make ye him drunken: for he magnified himself against the Lord: Moab also shall wallow in his vomit, and he also shall be in derision" (Jeremiah 48:26).

By reading the Scriptures we see that there are a number of things that go hand in hand with drunkenness: immorality, rebellion against God, the destruction of man. Is it any wonder that God hates drunkenness and puts a curse on the drunkard?

The more carefully I study the subject in the Bible, the stronger is my conviction that it is basically the product and not the individual that causes alcoholism. Read Jeremiah 13:13 again, and you will note that the prophecy says God is going to use drunkenness to bring destruction to the nation. He did not say He was going to make them all psycho-neurotic so that they would fall into the clutches of wine.

History reveals that sixteen civilizations have fallen because of drunkenness. When we see the tragic increase in alcoholism in America today we cannot but wonder whether God is going to use this means of bringing judgment against our great nation for turning against Him.

SHOULD THE CHRISTIAN ABSTAIN?

As an alcoholic I know what would happen to me, personally, if I took another drink. Of course, that is one of the reasons I practice abstinence.

But that is not the reason I believe in total abstinence for Christians.

A good case against using alcohol can be made by examining the results of drinking, but those facts are not necessarily enough. For example:

At any rescue mission anywhere in the country you can see, firsthand, what alcohol has done to men's minds and bodies. A visit to the squalid little skid-row mortuary just off Madison Street in Chicago where funerals are held every day for the victims of alcohol who have died on the street would give you a chilling view of the effects of drinking. The dirty, storefront funeral parlor rarely has a single mourner at their ten-minute services. A man from the nearby rescue mission may be there to say a word and offer prayer, but that is all.

A look at the case history files of the nearest rescue mission will reveal grim, painful stories of how alcohol destroys dignity and personal integrity. Men confess to stealing the groceries their wives have bought to feed their families (probably with the last money in the house) and selling them for a bottle of cheap wine. They have been known to steal the shoes from their children's feet for the same purpose.

I know from personal experience the agony and terror of delirium tremens, when the bed seems to shake so violently the alcoholic is afraid he will fall out; when he dozes into a half stupor-half sleep, only to be awakened to an entire room crawling with weird, writhing things so hideous they chill his blood; when he is so terrified he screams helplessly against them, certain he will die of fright.

But for some reason such stories are not effective in keeping a young person from alcohol or in getting a social drinker to stop. A mixture of pride and personal superiority makes the average individual think that such things happen only to others who are so weak they cannot control themselves or their liquor.

An article on teenage drinking in the August 13, 1985, issue of *Women's Day* states that it usually takes adults a number of years of heavy drinking to make them alcoholics, but many teens make the trip in a few short months. Most are smaller than adults and have considerably less body weight, which increases the effect of a given amount of alcohol dramatically. Many gulp their beer or wine or hard liquor hurriedly. The teens quoted said they drank to get drunk.

A certain research group found evidence that diet caused liver damage and liver damage increased one's susceptibility to alcoholism. In most cases cirrhosis of the liver is caused by drinking, but in Africa a high percentage of people had cirrhosis of the liver because of malnutrition.

The diet of the average teenager is so unbalanced he too can be suffering from a degree of malnutrition. Many eat no breakfast, bolt a hamburger, french fries, and a soft drink for lunch, and have a pizza for dinner. Without seeing any studies on the subject I have the feeling that diet has much to do with the rapidity with which many teenagers fall prey to alcoholism.

Temperance has long been taught in the schools, but a survey made by the state of Kansas on the effect of such teaching revealed some interesting facts. According to the questionnaires filled out by high school youngsters across Kansas, the schools' efforts to promote temperance had few lasting results.

Students were asked, "Where do you think the teaching of temperance is effective?"

The overwhelming majority replied that the temperance teaching they received in their church was the most effective. This means that we, as Christians, have both the greatest opportunity and the greatest responsibility in the matter.

Our teaching of abstinence can be most effective if we base it solidly upon a personal relationship to the Lord Jesus Christ. Although I have to tell drunks that there is no place in the Bible that says they shouldn't drink, there is strong scriptural basis for total abstinence for the Christian.

A study of drinking in the Word of God leads one to the discovery that there were two classes of people who were not to drink. Priests and kings were ordered to abstain from alcohol for a specific reason (Leviticus 10:8-11; Proverbs 31:4-5).

Priests were ordered not to drink during their course in the Temple so they could tell the difference between the good and the bad.

Kings and princes were not to drink for the same reason. They were to abstain from drinking so they could tell the difference between right and wrong and be fair in their judgment of the people who came before them.

The book of Revelation states that those who have accepted Christ as Savior are kings and priests: "And from Jesus Christ the faithful and trustworthy Witness, the First-born of the dead [that is, first to be brought back to life] and the Prince (Ruler) of the kings of the earth. To Him Who ever loves us and has once [for all] loosed and freed us from our sins by His own blood, . . . And formed us into a kingdom [a royal race], priests to His God and Father, to Him be the glory and the power and the majesty and the dominion throughout the ages and forever and ever. Amen, so be it" (Revelation 1:5-6, Amp.*).

The apostle Peter also says that we became kings and priests. We are members of a royal family. "But ye are a chosen generation, a royal priesthood, an holy nation, a peculiar people" (1 Peter 2:9).

Because of our salvation through faith in Christ we have become sons, the adopted sons of the King. As such we are members of the King's family, and the orders that went out to the kings and priests apply to us. We are not to drink so that we will have clear judgment and discernment as God's representatives in this world.

"As the Father hath sent me, so send I you," Jesus told His disciples (John 20:21). As Christians we are sent to witness, to teach the people. This is the responsibility of the believer. "Go ye therefore [into all the world], and teach," the Lord Jesus Christ instructed His disciples (Matthew 28:19). In order to teach we must know the difference between right and wrong.

*Amplified New Testament.

Therefore I believe that we as Christians are not to drink alcohol.

On one occasion after I presented this thesis to a youth group a young man got to his feet. "The Bible says that the priest isn't supposed to drink when he's in the Temple, but what about when he's outside the Temple? It doesn't mention that."

"That's true," I told him. "But the Bible also says, 'Ye are the temple of the living God' (2 Corinthians 6:16). As believers we are always living in God's temple. We are to think of ourselves as serving God daily in the temple of our bodies, and to do this we must so live as to be usable to Him."

The Christian does not drink because he knows the Lord Jesus Christ personally and is a member of His family. The Christian is a king and a priest, and the Bible specifically says that kings and priests are not to drink. The matter of total abstinence, then, depends upon our love for the Lord Jesus Christ.

How much do we love Him?

Part 2

Ways Others Can Help the Alcoholic

Every problem people face has a spiritual solution. The ever-increasing problem of alcoholism is no exception. God has provided a way of escape. Those who are trying to help alcoholics must believe this. Otherwise, counseling an alcoholic or dealing with a family member ensnared in alcohol addiction can be a frustrating experience. The situation is so complex, so staggering, that there seems to be no solution apart from the conviction that God has provided a way of escape.

The road to rehabilitation may be long and difficult, but there is hope. First we must come to understand the alcoholic and the product that has enslaved him. Then we must inform ourselves about the ways in which he can be helped. Whether we are working in a rescue mission, or as a pastor or counselor, or whether we suffer the alcohol addiction of one of our loved ones, there are definite ways we can help the alcoholic. We will consider these in detail in this section.

SEVEN
TAP THE RESOURCES OF PRAYER

A father had just stumbled home and was sprawled on the floor in a drunken stupor. His distraught wife knelt beside him, threw her body across his, and in anguish cried out in prayer. "God, deliver him from the power of drink. Make him a decent husband and father again. I commend him to Thee in the name of Christ!"

A widow with two small children, she had married this man after his first wife died, leaving him with three small children. For several years they were very happy—until drink began to get its claws into Clarence.

In time they were separated, and the wife, following the advice of well-meaning friends and going against her own judgment, divorced him. He went off into the never-never land of the alcoholic in a helpless, hopeless, self-centered search for one bottle after another.

It was twelve years before she saw Clarence again. This time he was sober and a respected member of the community. He was on the staff of the rescue mission where he had found Christ as his Savior. It was our privilege to remarry them.

"I prayed for Clarence's salvation for twelve years," she told me. "I knew he was going to become a Christian. I kept asking God to save him."

Three years or more before they met again and were remarried she heard that he had become a believer.

"My prayers changed," she continued. "I thanked God for saving him and delivering him from the power of drink. I started praying that we might be reunited if that was God's plan for our lives."

The first way to help the alcoholic is to pray for him. "You can do more than pray after you've prayed," S. D. Gordon says in his book *Quiet Talks on Prayer*, "but you cannot do more than pray until you have prayed."

There is no area in which this statement is more true than in working with the alcoholic. There is much that can be done for him, but we cannot successfully do anything until we have committed our loved one into the hands of the Lord.

"Our prayer," Mr. Gordon explains, "is God's opportunity to get into the world which shut Him out."

Put the alcoholic on your prayer list, and pray for him by name daily, believing that God is going to deliver him. The most powerful weapon we have is prayer. Because it is so powerful, we must know how to handle it.

Prayer is so important in dealing with the alcoholic because the alcoholic cannot be helped unless he wants to be. Before anything can be done for him, he must reach the place where he asks for help himself. We can only help him decide that he wants help and will cooperate with the help he gets. The first step in accomplishing this is through prayer.

There are a few simple ground rules we must understand and follow if our prayer lives are to be successful.

BE SURE YOU ARE A MEMBER OF GOD'S FAMILY

Prayer is a privilege and duty of the children of God.

When the disciples asked the Lord Jesus to teach them to pray, He said, "When ye pray, say, Our Father which art in heaven" (Luke 11:2).

If our prayers are going to be effective, we must first determine our relationship with the Lord Jesus Christ. Have we experienced a personal deliverance from sin through faith in Christ? Have we been born into the family of God? If we have, we know that we have a right to pray to God as our heavenly Father.

STAND ON GOD'S PROMISE TO ANSWER

Consider again what the Word of God has to say about prayer and answers to prayer in order that our faith might be strengthened.

"Listen to me! You can pray for anything, and if you believe, you have it; it's yours!" (Mark 11:24, TLB*).

"And so it is with prayer—keep on asking and you will keep on getting; keep on looking and you will keep on finding; knock and the door will be opened" (Luke 11:9, TLB).

We can know that God will hear and answer our cries for help because He has told us so in His Word. Always remember that nothing is impossible with God, no matter how hopeless the situation seems to be.

Art Lock was a rascal until he found Christ as his Savior.

"For twenty years my mother prayed for me fifteen hundred miles away in Lodi, California," he wrote. "In 1950 she prayed that God would send some other mother's lost, wayward son to her door so she could feed him, pray for him, and lead him to Christ in my place. . . . Seven times men came to her door, and she was able to lead them to Christ. Each time when the men were gone she prayed, 'Please, God, send someone to talk to my boy.'

"The seventh man was killed by a train the night after he knelt and accepted the Lord in her living room.

"That was in August, 1951 and—for some reason—he was the last man who came to her door. As Christmas approached, she asked God to send her a postcard telling her that I had been saved.

"December 24, 1951, my aunt brought the mail to

The Living Bible.

mother saying, 'There's nothing here except a dirty old postcard addressed to you. I can hardly read it.'

"Mother seized the card and read, 'Your prayers have been answered. I have been saved. I am coming home. Buster.' "

Art had been saved in prison in October of the same year after having been arrested for the two-hundredth time. A mother's prayer was answered.

"God does nothing but in answer to prayer," John Wesley said many, many years ago.

Make the Right Approach

The Scriptures speak of both public and private prayer. We need to observe both kinds as we pray for the alcoholic.

Private prayer, getting alone with God, should be a daily practice. It is by regular, private prayer that we keep ourselves in a right relationship with God so that He can answer our prayers. In private prayer we confess our outbursts of temper, our envy and jealousy and pride, and ask God to take them from us. It is as we confess our sins that God cleanses us and makes us suitable channels for answered prayer.

"Behold, the Lord's hand is not shortened, that it cannot save; neither his ear heavy, that it cannot hear: But your iniquities have separated between you and your God, and your sins have hid his face from you, that he will not hear" (Isaiah 59:1-2).

Sin in our lives will keep God from answering our prayers. If we expect to be heard and answered we must honestly search our hearts and lives to see if we have a right attitude. There is no better place to do this than in our private prayers and devotions.

Tom Hare, who was well known in America a few years ago as the Praying Plumber of Lisburn, Ireland, was speaking in a church when several women came to him and asked him to pray for their unsaved alcoholic husbands. That night on his knees he realized, even as he prayed, that the hearts of the women were wrong. The next day he called them together.

"You've asked me to pray for your husbands," he said, "but you have a selfish attitude. You want them sober so you'll have more money and an easier life. You're not truly interested in their salvation."

The women realized that what he said was true. They confessed their selfish reasons for wanting their husbands to give up alcohol. When they confessed that fact to God a wonderful thing happened. Their husbands, who hadn't been to church in years, began to attend the special meetings. One by one, they found Christ as their Savior. By the time the series of meetings was over, all those men had become Christians.

They began to meet for fellowship, forming a little chapter of Alcoholics Victorious. Each time they were together they spend a period interceding with God for the souls of their former drinking buddies. A number of them received Christ and stopped drinking, as well.

Just as that group of women had to examine themselves, confess the sin in their lives, and ask God to blot it out, so must we before God will work in the lives of our loved ones.

Public prayer is most commonly practiced in the prayer meeting at church. In public prayers, a group of Christians share mutual burdens and pray together for a given problem or a certain situation. In Matthew 18:19 Christ makes a special promise to answer the prayers of those who get together to petition Him for a certain purpose.

It has always seemed to me that there is a special blessing when we humble ourselves enough in a prayer meeting to ask for prayer for a loved one by name. Few people will remember to pray for an "unspoken prayer request" in the days to come, but many will be concerned and pray for the loved one or friend of a fellow believer.

"Nothing seemed to happen in the life of our wayward daughter who was rapidly becoming an alcoholic," a distraught father told me, "until I was so burdened in prayer meeting one night that I cried out to God for her by name. From that moment on there was a marked change—not in her: the change in her life came later. But the members of the church began to tell us that they were praying for her and for my wife and me. There was real concern in the congregation. The burden became easier to bear, and in time she gave her heart to Christ."

Both private and public prayer can be intercessory prayer. "God forbid that I should sin against the Lord in ceasing to pray for you" (1 Samuel 12:23). In this type of prayer we intercede before God for others. The Bible urges us to pray for one another. In the Old Testament, godly Samuel viewed failure to pray for the nation of Israel as a sin. The need of the nation was a call to prayer. The need of the alcoholic is our call to intercessory prayer. In intercessory prayer we make known before God all the details we know of a particular person or problem, and we ask Him to move in that particular situation.

I have found intercessory prayer a most valuable tool when counseling with the alcoholic. So often it is difficult for him to express himself. He has trouble saying what is on his mind and his heart. Very seldom do you get down to the very truth of the problem on the first or second interview.

But it is profitable to pray for that individual at every interview; to lift him into the hands of the Lord and petition God to deliver him. At the close of the interview, I reach out to shake hands with the individual. While I have his hand in mine I say, "Let's pray."

Often, surprising things happen. I find that sometimes the person completely breaks down after I have committed him and his problem to the Lord. When that happens I have an opportunity to get to the very crux of the matter. Often the individual will ask God for a new life through Jesus Christ.

So if God provides the opportunity for counseling with an alcoholic, don't forget to pray for him at the close of the interview.

In some cases the family of the alcoholic has a guilt complex. They ask themselves, "Have I done the right thing? Have I done all I could have done? Why did I lose my temper and talk so terribly that I drove him back to the bottle?" Those who have such feelings can and should have victory over them.

In the first place, most of the temper spectacles staged by the alcoholic's family come about only after grave provocation. It is not easy to live with an alcohol addict or to work with him. And we do have our human frailties which cause us, if pressed hard enough, to explode in fits of anger.

But there is no need to justify our actions. We can confess our sins and failures to God and be sure of His forgiveness, even as our alcoholic can have the past wiped away if he confesses his sin.

Whether we have failed or succeeded in the past makes no difference. We must start where we are and go on from there. If you have a guilt complex, bring it to the Lord and leave it there, and enjoy the freedom and peace that come with complete forgiveness.

Members of the alcoholic' s family often find, when they begin to pray for him, that in certain areas they have unknowingly and unwittingly made a contribution to the drinking of the individual. They also discover areas in which they too have been selfish and self-centered.

A certain husband and wife came to see me at my office in Omaha. The husband told me he had gone back to drinking after being free from it for some time. I explained that he had to turn his entire life over to God—that there was an area over which he did not have complete victory, a particular sore spot that caused him to explode into another drink. "You have to search your heart," I told him. "You must be honest with God and ask Him to deliver you."

His wife spoke up tearfully. "I have to pray, too. I haven't done the things he has done, but my sins are just as black. I have to turn my life completely over to God too."

That admission of guilt broke her husband. They fell on their knees and prayed together.

Up until the time I lost track of them several years later, they were living together happily. Their home was free from the awful curse of alcoholism.

BE WILLING TO BE GOD'S SUPPLY LINE

It is important that we constantly remember that we are channels of God's power. Our hearts are burdened because of the terrible curse that has taken hold of our alcoholic. We cry out to God. That sets the forces of almighty God to work. He sends His power by the Holy Spirit to us and through us to that individual.

We don't see this power radiating through us, and we can't feel it, but that is the way it works.

We may be sure God is interested in this problem. He loves this person more than we do. As we pray we cooperate with God in bringing His purposes to pass. We should not beg God, but after we've asked Him to bring deliverance to the individual, we should begin to thank Him that He is going to do what we have asked. We must believe with all our hearts that God is going to work and trust Him to do so.

This is not easy. We have been suffering for such a long while under the curse of alcoholism that we are impatient for God to work. We pray, and, when nothing happens immediately we begin to get discouraged, and our doubts grow.

A sort of chain reaction sets in. Discouragement causes us to fail to thank God that He is answering prayer. We get careless, then, about naming the individual before the Lord in prayer.

Times without number people have come into my office, their faces lined with weariness and doubt, who say something like this: "I've reached the place where I'm tired of praying. God isn't going to answer."

I know exactly how they feel. We all have to fight

against the sin of discouragement. The moment we become discouraged and stop thanking God ahead of time for answering our prayers and begin to neglect praying for the alcoholic we are so concerned about, we will lose our effectiveness. God has to turn His attention to us and work with us, moving in our hearts and lives by His Spirit to get us to see our sin.

Perhaps some other sin besides the lack of faith and discouragement is blocking the channel and hindering answers to our prayers—hatred, an unforgiving spirit, the wrong attitude.

During our years at the mission there were men we would just as soon have written off as hopeless so we would not have to work with them. I remember one particular fellow who felt that he had been cheated in the settlement of an accident claim. Because that happened he made up his mind that he wasn't going to work the rest of his life.

He was at the Open Door Mission when a crew from one of the local TV stations came down to do a program about the work. As was our policy, they were free to interview anyone there without the presence of mission personnel. This man was one of those who was interviewed.

A couple of days later the TV producer called me to his office and asked me to listen to the tape. All the man's bitterness poured out in a tirade against me personally, the Open Door Mission in particular, and rescue missions in general.

I was furious.

Then God convicted me of my attitude toward him. I confessed it and began to pray that God would deliver him from the bonds of sin. But I still didn't think I wanted to have any part of working with him.

God dealt with me about that, too. I had confessed my wrong attitude and was praying for the man's salvation, but I am not sure I really wanted what I was praying for. At any rate, I didn't want it badly enough to be willing to deal with the man myself. I began to pray that if God wanted me to talk with him He would send him around again.

God did just that.

It wasn't easy for me when the man came into my office for counseling. The bitterness and hatred I thought I had put aside welled up within me. My feelings were a reaction to the man's warped philosophy that the world owed him a living and he wasn't going to work another day in his life. I strongly believe that a man should not eat if he does not work.

Once more I had to confess to God my unwillingness to witness to him and to ask Him for the victory I needed to talk intelligently with this man. Until that moment I hadn't honestly wanted what I had been praying for.

I wish I could say that he accepted Christ as his Savior, but to my knowledge that hasn't happened. He is working and holding down a job, however, and until I left Omaha and saw him no more, our relationship was good. We still pray for him, confident that one day he is going to receive Christ.

DON'T FORGET TO ASK

In a way it seems strange that we must ask God before He will answer, but that is another principle of prayer. It is true that God knows our every need, even before we ask. It is also true that He says we should ask in order to receive. "And all things, whatsoever ye shall ask in prayer, believing, ye shall receive" (Matthew 21:22). That is a positive promise from God. If we ask, we are going to receive. So we must ask.

But we must know what we are asking for. Is what we want according to God's will? I am quite sure that is the reason our blessed Lord insists that we talk these things over with Him. As we do, we submit our wills to His will. And we present with confidence any petition that is according to His will.

Not long ago a business acquaintance was having some difficult business problems. I asked if he had ever talked to God about it.

"I'm not sure I understand what you mean."

"If you went to a bank to get a loan you'd talk it over with the banker, wouldn't you? You would have to give him a list of your assets and liabilities. You'd have to explain to him the business potential you saw in the future. In short, you would have to take the banker into your confidence. He would need to know certain things about you and your business if he were to make you a business loan. Isn't that true?"

"I suppose so."

"That's what God means when He tells us to ask Him for things in prayer," I continued. "Why don't you get your books out and make up a statement and read it before God and let Him in on your business? Then ask God for the things you need—money, better employee relations, a better location, or any other need. Talk your problems over with God."

When I walked into his office a month or so later, he reminded me of our conversation.

"I did just what you suggested," he said. "I got my books and made my statement and read it off before God. You know, it is wonderful the way things have happened and how God is managing this business and making it a success."

Perhaps you need to do the same in praying for your alcoholic.

EXPECT AN ANSWER

Are you honestly expecting an answer? Or have you allowed doubts to cloud your heart so you go through the motions of prayer without any real assurance that God even hears? Doubt is like a canker, a great hindrance to prayer. Doubt is sin and must be judged and confessed.

The chief reason we doubt is that we don't appreciate the God we are dealing with. Our minds accept that God is great, that He is all-powerful, that He can change the life of an individual or the course of any series of circumstances.

But our hearts won't believe it. If they did, doubts

would not destroy our peace of mind and blight our prayer life.

We must stop and consider how great God is!

"What heathen god can give us rain? Who but you alone, O Lord our God, can do such things as this? Therefore we will wait for you to help us" (Jeremiah 14:22, TLB).

He created the heaven and the earth out of nothing. The mountains and deserts and mighty oceans are His handiwork. He orders the affairs of men. He moves against nations to work out His will.

This is the God to whom we pray. This is the God who urges us to make our requests known to Him. "Do not be anxious about anything, but in everything, by prayer and petition, with thanksgiving, present your requests to God. And the peace of God, which transcends all understanding, will guard your hearts and your minds in Christ Jesus" (Philippians 4:6-7, NIV).

How can we doubt our mighty, all-powerful God?

Statistics show that an alcoholic in his twenties is more difficult to reach than one who is thirty-five or forty years old. They say the alcoholic who has been jailed for drunkenness a number of times is a better risk than the alcoholic who has been jailed for some criminal offense. Such a man, they say, seldom comes to seek help.

And with 75 percent of all crime committed by individuals who are under the influence of alcohol, we can safely conclude that there are a lot of such men around. Some have been released from prison on parole. Humanly speaking, such men appear to be hopeless, but they aren't. God makes the difference.

Why God would want to answer the prayers of weaklings like us I do not know, but how I praise Him that he does.

"But God hath chosen the foolish things of the world to confound the wise; and God hath chosen the weak things of the world to confound the things which are mighty, and base things of the world, and things which are despised, hath God chosen, yea, and things which are not, to bring to nought things that are" (1 Corinthians 1:27-28).

God can take nothing and use it to bring to nought that which is. How comforting that should be to each of us who is praying for an alcoholic. It doesn't make any difference how long the individual has been addicted to alcohol or how bad the situation is. God is on the throne. He is able to take that helpless, hopeless individual and restore him completely as a useful member of society.

Time after time during my thirty years in the ministry of rescue I have seen God work in that way. I am a product of His redeeming power.

Prayer does change people!

EIGHT
PRESENT THE GOSPEL

I know what the gospel of Christ was able to do for me when I was in that Texas prison in 1948. I know what He is doing in my life every day. I have seen how He has worked in the lives of men and women in all avenues of society, snatching them from the relentless grip of alcohol addiction and setting them free.

"Religion can be a tremendous force in the rehabilitation of an alcoholic," said Phyllis Snyder of Chicago's highly successful Alcoholic Treatment Center.

Paul uses even stronger terms: "The gospel of Christ . . . is the power of God unto salvation to everyone that believeth; to the Jew first and also to the Greek" (Romans 1:16).

God's Way Is Basic

Dr. E. M. Jellinek, who was one of the world's foremost experts in the field of alcoholism, noted in his study on alcohol addiction and chronic alcoholism that religious security and standards rate highly in overcoming alcoholism.

A pamphlet on the subject published by the Yale Center of Alcohol Studies reaches the same conclusion. "The number of addictive drinkers who have been helped to attain permanent abstinence by the means of religious approaches is probably far greater than is usually accepted."

Clifford J. Earle, author of *How to Help an Alcoholic*, says, "Religion is a major aid in the treatment of alcoholism. Christ is not just another alcoholic therapy, however, as though one could choose between a religious or a psychiatric treatment. Instead it is an approach that takes into account the spiritual aspects of personality and religious resources for successful living."

We can only stand back and wonder at the grace of God.

WHERE DO WE BEGIN?

When we first consider the problem of alcoholism and make an attempt to understand the alcoholic, we are apt to be overwhelmed. The problem is so bewildering and has so many ramifications we scarcely know where to begin. We feel as though we are in a maze and find it easy to forget that the most important thing we can do for the alcoholic is to present Christ to him.

To be sure it isn't always possible to preach the gospel to every man on every occasion. You can't present Christ to him effectively if he is in a drunken stupor or needs medical attention. But we must always keep our attention focused on this one fact: the most important thing we can do for the alcohol addict is to speak to him of Christ at the earliest possible moment.

Garland Thompson, the founder and superintendent of the Open Door Mission in Omaha for a number of years, taught me this. He had never been an alcoholic, nor had he made a special study of alcoholism. His entire life had been devoted to prayer and personal witnessing.

I have seen Garland put an arm around a man who was too drunk to talk, telling him that God loves him and praying for him before he sent him on his way to sober up or perhaps to get medical attention. I had the privilege of talking to some of those same men after they were won to Christ.

"Know what set me to thinking?" they would tell me gratefully. "It was Garland Thompson putting his arm around me and telling me that God loves me and because He loves me, you guys here at the mission were going to help me. I was pretty drunk, but that got through."

It was Christ who worked the victory in the lives of such men (and women), freeing them from alcoholism. In my own experience, it was the gospel of the Lord Jesus Christ that got hold of me after everything else had failed. If your alcoholic is to be delivered, you must present the gospel to him.

That may not always be easy. A good friend of mine with an alcoholic brother found that to be true. "I've had all of you I can take!" his brother snarled at him. "Now leave me alone!"

An attorney discouraged him when he mentioned trying to get help for his brother through the gospel. The attorney scornfully said, "If the psychiatrists and trained people at the state hospital weren't able to help him, I'm sure your religious friend wouldn't be able to do anything for him."

As the "religious friend," I wasn't able to help personally, but I was able to point the young alcoholic to the One who could solve all his problems. He became a stalwart Christian.

GOD'S LOVE CHANGES LIVES

Working with alcoholics is not the most enjoyable part of a pastor's ministry. The alcoholic is often difficult, surly, and uncooperative. Usually he thinks that anyone who tries to help him is a personal enemy. He is secretive, untruthful, and suspicious, and is apt to be involved in immorality, the writing of bad checks, and gambling. His excessive and compulsive drinking has deeply hurt and affected the lives of—on the average—five innocent persons. He has become a blight on his family and his community.

The average pastor has gone through some difficult experiences with alcoholics—experiences similar to those I have had.

On one occasion I was called to the home of a man who had fallen against the French doors in his living room. His arms were badly cut when they went through the glass, and he was standing in the middle of the room, blood running in puddles on the white rug. He was in a drunken rage. His terrified daughters were sobbing in the bedroom, and his wife was shouting at him angrily, scarcely mindful of the fact that he had been seriously hurt.

Another time I was called to the home of a lovely family in a very nice neighborhood. What I found was anything but lovely. The older son, who had lost his wife because of alcoholism, seemed determined to drink himself to death. The stench in the room he had refused to leave for more than a week was terrible, and the filth was something I can't put into words. It wasn't easy to view that situation—the hurt that dimmed his Christian mother's eyes and the mute agony on the face of his Christian sister.

When we find ourselves in such a situation it is often difficult to remember that God is all-powerful and that Jesus Christ, through the power of the gospel, can change the life of a man.

Pastors as well as mission workers need to continually be aware of the fact that God does love the alcoholic and that we, who are His ambassadors, must love the alcoholic, too.

"But God commendeth his love toward us, in that, while we were yet sinners, Christ died for us" (Romans 5:8). We need to be reminded that men and women are saved from the horrors of alcoholism and are brought to a place of respectability and service by the gospel of Christ.

Stan Collie was such a man. He had degenerated to the point where, at forty years of age, he allowed his wife and six children to go hungry so he could have something to drink. On Saturday nights his wife and two of the older youngsters would go down to the business district of their little northern Saskatchewan community to pick him out of the gutter and pull him home in a coaster wagon.

Then Christ got hold of him. His life was transformed. He began to witness to others and soon developed a great burden for the Indian people who lived in the Canadian north. Today he is known as the founder of the Northern Canada Evangelical Mission, an organization that has become a great force for God with almost two hundred missionaries all across Canada. We should look upon each man as an opportunity.

COUNSELING TAKES TIME

Often pastors are reluctant to work with the alcoholic because of the time it requires. We feel there is so much to do in seeing that the various church activities run smoothly and the needs of the rest of the congregation are met that we can't devote the time to one individual.

"You have to throw the clock away when you're dealing with the alcoholic," Charles Morey of the Chicago Christian Industrial League said. "It is probably the most time-consuming type of counseling most of us will ever do."

Some pastors solve the problem by forming a team of concerned men within the church to work with the individual alcohol addict and help him out of alcoholism. We will go into that in greater detail in the chapter on fellowship.

CHRISTIANITY IS A WAY OF LIFE

I have found that an alcoholic may have to go all the way to the bottom, and sometimes onto skid row, before he will believe because he has not seen the Christian life demonstrated in those around him.

"Everyone talks a good game when it comes to this Christian life," one alcoholic said to me with keen perception, "but I don't see anyone playing it very well."

There are times when I cannot help wondering if such failure in Christian living isn't the biggest hindrance some alcoholics have to face.

One such situation came to us while I was at the mission. The husband—we'll call him Pete—had a relationship with his church but had not taken Christ as his Savior. The wife, Sue, was a Christian; she had had some Bible training and had been a home missionary for several years before their marriage. But she was one of those strong-willed, opinionated women who has to have everything her own way. It wasn't long after they were married that she began to go to work on Pete. By that time he had become an alcoholic and came to me for counseling. I tried to talk to him about the things of the Lord, but it was difficult for him to understand what I was talking about.

Since 85 percent of all alcoholics still have a home and a family, it is important that a counselor take the entire family into consideration. That is what I did with Pete and Sue.

We soon discovered that during the time Pete fell into drinking Sue had a very definite spiritual lack—a lack of dependency upon the Lord. She was a Christian, able to understand salvation. In fact, she was well versed in the Bible and domineered in their family devotions. She harped so much on salvation that Pete rebelled against her and the Christ she talked so much about. She seemed to have no understanding of how to live a victorious Christian life. Nor did she seem to know that God could give her victory over her problems.

"I might not know much about the Bible," Pete told me, "but I do know this. If I'm going to be free from alcoholism, I've got to have something better than Sue has. As a matter of fact, if what she's got is religion, I know that religion is not the answer to my problem."

After a time we were able to help him to see things in their right perspective, and he came to a saving knowledge of the Lord Jesus Christ.

He began to live the Christian life, took over the leadership in their home, and gave the Word of God its rightful place, as he should have done all along. Then he was able to help his very weak, insecure wife in a number of areas of her life. She is a better Christian today because her husband knows the Lord.

When we talk with an alcoholic about the Lord Jesus Christ, we must be very careful that we ourselves understand that Christianity is a way of life, not a theology to be expounded.

We can teach Sunday school, harp continually on religion, keep a Bible in the most prominent place in the home, and have devotions regularly. Yet if we are not living victorious Christian lives, we cannot hope to reach our alcoholic.

"What you are," Emerson wrote many years ago, "speaks so loudly I cannot hear a word you say."

We should prayerfully strive to live in such a way that the alcoholic will look at us and say to himself, "I want what that person has."

CHRISTIANITY IS A NEW LIFE

We should remind the alcoholic who is making a profession of faith that faith in Christ means a new life. "Therefore if any man be in Christ, he is a new creature: old things are passed away; behold, all things are become new" (2 Corinthians 5:17).

Salvation is a ticket to heaven, that is true. Much of the New Testament deals with salvation, and some of the most important passages of Scripture explain how one might obtain it. We cannot minimize the importance of salvation. Yet all too often we have made it the place where our Christian experience ends, and it should be nothing of the sort. When a person is saved, he is born again. This new birth marks the beginning of a new and entirely different life. That new life must grow and develop and mature.

That truth presents a tremendous appeal to the alcoholic. He has made such a terrible mess of his old life that he has reached the end of the road. The dirty, tangled skein of his past could never be untangled and knit into anything worthwhile. A new life is the only answer for his situation.

"And along with this gift comes the realization that God wants us to turn from godless living and from sinful pleasures and to live good, God-fearing lives day after day, looking forward to that wonderful time we've been expecting, when his glory shall be seen—the glory of our great God and Savior Jesus Christ. He died under God's judgment against our sins, so that he could rescue us from constant falling into sin and make us his very own people, with cleansed hearts and real enthusiasm for doing kind things for others" (Titus 2:12-14, TLB).

The grace of God provides more than deliverance from the punishment our sins deserved, more than a leisurely journey into heaven. God's grace gives the believing sinner a completely new life.

When we talk with a new Christian it is wise to talk with him about taking a personal inventory, listing his bad and good qualities and asking God to take over in the areas where he needs help.

We should also urge him to feed on God's Word and to pray every morning. The best advice ever given to me was written on a postcard by a Christian who belonged to the Gideons. He wrote, "Spend fifteen minutes a day reading your Bible and fifteen minutes a day in prayer. If you start your day that way, you'll keep true to the Lord and grow in Him."

When we present the gospel of the Lord Jesus Christ to the individual we must be careful not to present a limited view of salvation. When we present the truth that Christianity is a new life, we give the alcoholic something to cling to. He will see that God is genuinely interested in him and will provide him with all that he needs. God has given him a new life that can be molded and shaped after Christ.

What a glorious hope!

NINE

PROVIDE FELLOWSHIP

THE NEED FOR FELLOWSHIP

It is hard to overemphasize the importance of fellowship to the alcoholic. Yet sometimes it seems impossible to give him what he needs—communion, intimacy, joint interests and feelings with those he loves. It is not easy for those involved with an alcoholic to provide fellowship.

How does a wife who has been beaten in a brutish, drunken rage forget such treatment? How does she put aside the ugly fact of her husband's infidelity? Can a father forget that his children have been neglected and abused? That the house is dirty because of his wife's drinking? Can a pastor or a counselor ignore the fact that an individual can cause so much anguish to so many innocent people?

Yet Alcoholics Anonymous, Alcoholics Victorious, friends, family, and the church are all involved in offering fellowship to the recovering alcoholic. No matter how difficult it is, we must provide fellowship for our alcoholic loved one if we are to help him to sobriety.

AA's approach can give us guidelines for our attempts at providing fellowship. In those programs, fellowship is offered but is never forced on the individual. If he wants it, the group stands ready to help him. If he doesn't, they accept the fact that there is nothing they can do at that particular time.

When a call from an alcoholic comes in, one or two

volunteers call on him (or her) to talk. They tell him about the program, what it has done for them, and what it can do for him. They don't berate him. They don't sulk and refuse to talk. They offer him fellowship. It is entirely up to him to accept their fellowship or not.

If he wants help, they will try to help him in every way possible. If medical care or hospitalization is necessary, they will try to get it for him. They will do what they can to help him through the awful throes of alcohol withdrawal.

They will invite him to a meeting. If he comes, he will be welcomed and will be made to feel at home. If he continues to respond, they will be able to help him.

Alcoholics Victorious is similar to Alcoholics Anonymous, offering the same sort of fellowship with the added help of strong Christian direction. It is a Christ-centered program and very often a church-centered program.

The individual needs fellowship in every area of life, however. Organizations like AA or AV can help lead an alcoholic to recovery, but his success is often hinged on the fellowship of those closest to him—a pastor or counselor, church members, and most importantly the members of his family.

Those are the people who must understand his problem and realize that he is suffering from addiction. They must help to create an atmosphere of fellowship for him and encourage him to desire sobriety more than alcohol. They must offer him respect and dignity and the opportunity to take his place as a respected member of society again.

THE SOURCE OF FELLOWSHIP

If we are to offer fellowship to an individual who has such a warped, self-centered personality that he has been living only for another drink, we need something outside ourselves to enable us to do it. We need a strong, abiding faith in Christ and the strength He can give.

When I was on the counseling staff at the Nebraska State Penitentiary, a certain prisoner asked to see me. I was given his case history. All the crimes he had been convicted of were listed, including the offense for which he was sentenced the last time.

What a character this guy is! I thought as I read it.

Yet, as I talked with him, he seemed sincere in his desire for help, and I had the privilege of leading him to personally acknowledge Christ as his Savior. As I watched him leave the room after the interview, I said to myself, *I wonder if he'll make it.*

Instantly the Lord rebuked me, and I had to ask myself, *How did you make it? You were in prison when you accepted Christ. Your record might not have been as long as this fellow's, but it was just as black. You were no better than he was. How did you make it?*

There is only one answer. I made it because God took over my life. He gave me the encouragement and strength I needed. He sent concerned Christians to help me. He would do the same with this individual.

Whenever I am faced with a difficult case, I am constantly reminded that nothing is too hard for the Lord, "who will have all men to be saved, and to come unto the knowledge of the truth" (1 Timothy 2:4).

We must remember that God is interested in every individual and that with His help we can offer fellowship to our alcoholic.

It is generally accepted that it takes an alcoholic to help an alcoholic. Although I personally have suffered from alcohol addiction, I do not have rapport with the alcoholic because of that. Garland Thompson had rapport with the men who came stumbling into the mission, and to my knowledge he had never taken a drink in his life.

We can have rapport with the alcoholic because we too have been separated from God by sin. And we have been delivered by Christ from our sin, even as he can be delivered by Christ.

We must hold before the alcoholic the truth that

Christ is vitally interested in the sinner. "And Jesus . . . said unto them, They that are whole need not a physician; but they that are sick. I came not to call the righteous, but sinners to repentance" (Luke 5:31-32).

We cannot isolate alcoholism as something ugly and almost unforgivable. We must see it as a part of the universal problem of sin. Once that is clear, we see our alcoholic as one who has the same problem with sin that we had. We see him as a sinner who needs deliverance from a sinful nature, who needs to be born again into a new life through Jesus Christ our Lord.

As a result, we no longer approach the problem of offering fellowship to him as a fearful thing. We no longer see him as a hideous person who brings grief and hurt to all of those who love him. We simply see him as a sinner in need of a deliverer. When we see his problem in that light, we are no longer afraid to attempt to cope with it.

THE SAMARITAN PRINCIPLE

The road from Jerusalem to Jericho was rocky and dangerous, a favorite lurking place for roving bands of thieves. The nameless traveler in the story of the Good Samaritan fell into the hands of such a band. They beat him, stripped off his clothes, and robbed him, leaving him half dead.

Today's alcoholic is also traveling a rough and rocky road. The thieves of alcoholic beverages have robbed him of his job, his home, and his family and stripped him of his self-respect. He has few friends in a world that condemns him because of his addiction.

In the Bible story, when the Good Samaritan came along, he had compassion for the man who had been so shamefully treated. Sorrow for the suffering of this poor fellow touched his heart. He had such concern and love that he did something about it.

We too must have the compassion and love the Good Samaritan showed if we are going to offer effective fellowship to our alcoholic. When we first see this poor, broken hulk there is a good possibility that he will need medical attention. We may have to see that he is treated by a doctor and possibly even hospitalized or taken to a treatment center. Often in treatment centers and rescue missions the individual must go through a long period of physical adjustment before any spiritual or mental therapy can be given.

The next thing the Samaritan did was to put the injured man on his own mount and take him to the inn, where he asked that the injured man be cared for. The Samaritan became personally involved by dressing the injured man's wounds, by taking him to the inn, and by offering payment for his care until he returned.

I shall never forget the first alcoholic I worked with after entering the ministry. He would come to the parsonage at two or three in the morning and get us out of bed. One night, by the time I got him steady enough to take him home and put him to bed, it was five in the morning. I was disgusted. I knelt in my study and talked with the Lord about him.

"I'm never going to have anything more to do with this fellow, Lord. He won't assume any of the responsibilities of his business or do anything his family asks him to do. He won't do anything I ask him to. He won't respond to the gospel. I'm through with him!"

Then a still, small voice seemed to speak to me. "Jerry, you're going to have John on your back until he is free." That is exactly the way it worked out.

When we work with the alcoholic we must work with him on an individual basis—as one person to another. We must not weaken or falter until he is delivered from his addiction.

Not only is it difficult to offer fellowship to our alcoholic, it costs something. Like the Good Samaritan, we must be willing to pay the price in time, money, and our own personal convenience. The price paid will seem small compared to the joy of seeing our alcoholic delivered from his chains and restored to a place of respect and dignity in the family, church, and community.

HINDRANCES TO FELLOWSHIP

Fellowship must be a team project if our alcoholic is to be helped to a life of total abstinence and permanent sobriety. It must come from the family, the church, friends, and associates. The first place the alcoholic should expect fellowship—at home—is usually the last place it is offered.

I have heard the indignant cries of those who have been hurt so deeply by their alcoholic loved one. "How can I offer fellowship to him when he has hurt me so much?"

The answer is found in the reply of the disciples when Christ told them they should forgive a person who had sinned against them seventy times seven.

"Lord, increase our faith" (Luke 17:4).

We cannot forgive enough to take such an individual back into fellowship without the help and strength that comes from God.

Marty Mann, founder of the national Council on Alcoholism, wrote from personal experience in her book *Marty Mann's New Primer on Alcoholism*. One chapter is called "Home Treatment."

> The "Home treatment" can be divided into two main categories, words and actions, or talk and behavior. Talk usually goes on for some time before behavior begins to bear it out. Then it continues right along side the behavior. For purposes of clarity we will follow the line of talk through to its bitter end before taking up the behavior which usually joins it midway.
>
> Talk, to someone whose drinking is beginning to create problems, usually begins with "sweet reasonableness." An effort is made at friendly discussion on what drinking is doing to the drinker (such as his "lack of judgment" and "thoughtfulness"), leading up to what it is doing to his family, at which time it is apt to become a trifle acid, and sometimes ends in an all-out row. Never-

theless, the effort to discuss the matter "reasonably" is renewed over and over again, despite the fact that as time goes on it seems to lead more and more swiftly to acrimonious dispute or cold anger. The alcoholic soon calls this nagging. . . .

Emotional appeals are another form of talk frequently used. "How can you do this to me?"; "Doesn't my love mean anything to you?" "How can you do this to the children" or "to yourself?" These point the finger of shame and blame at the alcoholic, increasing his already acute sense of guilt, and giving him another excuse to drink more, in order to "forget.". . .

Neither the emotional appeal nor the morality lecture ever seems to do the slightest good in bringing an alcoholic to seek help.[1]

Mrs. Mann goes on to state that promises and coaxing might appear to have some success at the time, but it is only temporary. Extracting a promise from an alcoholic is a waste of time. By this time, he probably couldn't keep it if he wanted to.

The wife or husband will usually advance to threatening to have the alcoholic jailed or committed to an institution, but that doesn't do any good either.

I have had many distraught spouses come into my office whose desperate stories follow the pattern so ably outlined by Mrs. Mann.

The behavior that goes with the talk is substantially the same. The alcoholic's spouse hides the liquor that is kept in the house, locks it up, or even pours it out.

"This usually proves a futile gesture," Mrs. Mann goes on, "for the alcoholic then sets his really remarkable ingenuity to getting more in, or getting himself out of the house and to the nearest source of supply. It must be remembered that to him, his need is desperate and overwhelming; it brooks no interference and sets up in him the blind courage of a charging bull, plus all the cunning and

1. Marty Mann, *Marty Mann's New Primer on Alcoholism* (New York: Holt, Rhinehart & Winston, 1981).

cleverness of a skilled second-story man."

There are other defense mechanisms—the withholding of money, or perhaps even reporting the tavern to the authorities for serving the alcoholic when he is already intoxicated. But these things are rarely effective. By this time the alcoholic is far gone and badly in need of treatment.

We who have had any dealings with alcoholics know how futile the type of home treatment just described actually is. We have tried it with many and varied innovations of our own. We know it doesn't work.

How, then, can we help?

HELP FOR FELLOWSHIP

The fellowship of the family is very important in the alcohol addict's recovery. Still, although we may want desperately to do everything necessary in order to help, we may be afraid it isn't going to work out.

Fear is very natural under such circumstances. We are afraid our alcoholic is going to take another drink. We are afraid he will lie to us again. We are even afraid that he is lying to us now. If he should be gone half an hour longer than we think he should be, we immediately begin to believe the worst.

But if we are going to help him, we have to take advantage of every sober moment. In that sober moment we must accept him as a normal individual; we must accept him into the family circle and routine.

To do that consistantly can be frustrating and takes its toll on us spiritually, mentally, and physically. If we are going to help our alcoholic, we must first get help for ourselves.

When we see a member of our family moving progressively down the seven steps to chronic alcoholism, we should talk with our minister, preferably, or another Christian in whom we have confidence, not necessarily to see what can be done for our alcoholic but to help us to get a right heart in meeting the problem. We need to be sure our faith in the Lord Jesus Christ is firm. We need to be sure that we have a forgiving spirit, even to the point of forgiving seventy times seven times. We must be certain that our personal relationship with Christ is such that it will allow us to take our troubled heart and mind and present them to Him to receive the assurance and strength we need to carry on.

Then we must use the ability and wisdom God gives us to be a help and not a stumbling block if we are to see our alcoholic make a recovery.

TEN
RELY ON GOD'S HELP

The Scriptures tell us that perfect love casts out fear. We must first love our Lord and Savior, Jesus Christ. As we love Him, we will be able to express love to our alcoholic and to trust his present sobriety.

Fear can carry within it the seeds of destruction.

If we are going to help our alcoholic, we must put fear aside and enter into normal activities with him, guiding him into associations with the kind of friends who will help rather hinder.

There is another factor that, unpleasant as it is, must be considered. Until our alcoholic is set completely free from the power of alcohol, there is a good probability that he or she will go on another drunk. Even if that happens, we must conduct ourselves in such a way that it does not interfere with our regular, normal home life. This may be one of the most difficult things we have to do.

Going ahead with a normal life will help make it possible for us to have the right frame of mind so we will want to continue to help our alcoholic without rancor or bitterness.

PSALM 37—THE THERAPY PSALM

I will never forget the first time I used this psalm in my efforts to rehabilitate those who were dominated by alcohol. It was many years ago when I was holding my first rehab program in the basement of our Omaha, Nebraska, home.

One of the fellows I was counseling had made a successful recovery from alcohol addiction and was trying desperately to reestablish himself with his wife and his nine-year-old daughter in Pennslyvania. It was Christmas, and he had sent his daughter a doll and his wife some money.

His wife sent the doll back but kept the money. "Neither Amy or I want to have anything to do with you," she wrote acidly. "You've completely destroyed any love either of us ever had for you."

He was crushed as he handed me the note.

"Why don't you read the thirty-seventh psalm?" I suggested. "Read it over and over until the truth of it begins to penetrate your heart and life."

A few minutes later I saw Art reading the psalm. Tears were running down his face as God spoke to his heart, healing his soul. God used that psalm like a rope to pull him out of his deep depression.

The first verse of Psalm 37 says, "Fret not thyself because of evil doers." The seventh verse says, "Fret not thyself because of him who prospereth in his way, because of the man who bringeth wicked devices to pass." And in the eighth verse, "Fret not thyself in any wise to do evil."

Going back to the second verse we are told, "For they shall soon be cut down like the grass, and wither as the green herb." Verses nine and ten continue the thought. "For evildoers shall be cut off: but those that wait upon the Lord, they shall inherit the earth. For yet a little while, and the wicked shall not be: yea, thou shalt diligently consider his place, and it shall not be."

These verses are especially beneficial for the alcoholic's family. We have been disappointed by him so many times that we have a tendency to fret. He doesn't seem to be paying any attention to us or our efforts to help. He continues to drink, and things seem to be going so well with him that he doesn't seriously concern himself with leaving alcohol alone.

We must remember that God tells us not to fret—that He will handle the matter. He will bring the alcoholic to the place where he will reach bottom—where the only way he can look will be up—to Him.

"Trust in the Lord and do good; so shalt thou dwell in the land, and verily thou shalt be fed" (Psalm 37:3). Our trust should be in God and in Him alone. It is fine to use groups for fellowship, but our trust must be in God. I have met many men and women who have placed their trust in one group or another. To place such faith in a group of people is wrong and most often results in failure at some point along the line.

People may turn their backs on us in a time of need. They may be unfair, criticize us, or do something else to shatter our faith in them.

God will never fail us. He will never stumble or turn His back on us in our time of need. When we place our trust in Him we are on solid ground. To trust man is to place our feet on shifting sand.

I found that out when I walked out of the State Penitentiary in Texas and had to face a world that knew me as a complete failure. As I laid hold on the Lord and trusted Him, He brought back my wife and family. And He established me in a job. From that job He took me to another job and then to the sort of job I had always dreamed of.

Even as a boy I had wanted a job on a newspaper but had never been able to make it. God gave me a position on the paper in Lamar, Colorado. I had reached the pinnacle of success. As far as I was concerned, I would be on that paper for the rest of my life.

Then God tapped me on the shoulder and told me He had something else for me. He took me out of the newspaper and into the ministry.

He taught me the meaning of Psalm 37:4. "Delight thyself also in the Lord; and he shall give thee the desires of thine heart."

I found out what it meant to be happy in the Lord and to be at peace.

I thought I was having a good time when I was drinking, but I soon found that I wasn't. I was in rebellion against life itself. I didn't know what it was to be happy and peaceful until I confessed my sin and put my trust in Christ Jesus. And I ruined the peace and happiness of my wife with my drinking.

The fifth verse was one that I soon learned had a special meaning for me. "Commit thy way unto the Lord; trust also in him; and he shall bring it to pass." The next verses also gave me strength and encouragement. "And he shall bring forth thy righteousness as the light, and thy judgment as the noonday."

Shortly after Greta accepted me back into our home, I bought a plaque, which I hung in our bedroom. It said, "God will give His best to those that leave the choice to Him." But I don't think I really looked at that plaque until one morning when I realized I was in deep trouble. I had restitution to make and a family to support. I had made some serious business mistakes that had put me deeply into debt, and I didn't know how to explain everything to my wife. I could almost hear her say, "Here we go again."

I turned to the fifth and sixth verses of the thirty-seventh psalm and read them carefully. They spoke to my heart as they never had before. Those verses had the advice I needed. I committed my way to the Lord, and He began to work out my problems. It wasn't an easy road, but I was on my way, one painful step at a time.

The seventh verse is particularly helpful to an alcoholic and his family. "Rest in the Lord, and wait patiently for him." And Psalm 62:1 goes along with it to complete the rest of the promise. "Truly my soul waiteth upon God: from him cometh my salvation."

Anyone with an alcoholic in the family knows much about waiting. You are experienced in waiting for your alcoholic to change, waiting for an opportunity to speak a word to him or her, waiting for things to be different.

God knows all about our waiting. He knows how difficult it is when we are dealing with problem people or are trying to recover from a problem such as alcoholism. He provides rest and strength to be kind and loving—if we will only trust Him.

Psalm 62:1 also tells us that God loves us right where we are.

I was in a prison cell when God found me and I confessed my sin and accepted Christ as my Savior. I hadn't changed. I was still the same rebellious character I had always been—with one important exception. I wanted to get away from the awfulness of myself.

I turned in the Bible to John 10:10. "I am come that they might have life, and that they might have it more abundantly." I said, "Lord, if that is what You have for me, that is what I want." In that moment I entered into God's salvation. I didn't understand it then. I still don't. But I had become a new creature in Christ Jesus.

No matter how badly you want to help your alcoholic loved one, you can't do anything unless you are a child of God. You must have the strength and power that God can give you. He wants to share it with you and begins when you receive Him as your Savior.

"But the meek shall inherit the earth; and shall delight themselves in the abundance of peace. . . . A little that the righteous man hath is better than the riches of many wicked. For the arms of the wicked shall be broken: but the Lord upholdeth the righteous. The Lord knoweth the days of the upright: and their inheritance shall be for ever. They shall not be ashamed in the evil time: and in the days of famine they shall be satisfied" (Psalm 37:11, 16-19).

What a promise God has for us. He assures us that He will see us through the lean times, even when there is not enough food in the house. He will take care of us.

In the twenty-first verse He tells us that He wants us to be giving—to share with others. I am firmly convinced that He will not provide us with the solution to our problems until we are willing to share His love with others.

Psalm 37:31 says, "The law of his God is in his heart; none of his steps shall slide." That tells us that we must take time to be with the Lord on a daily basis, hiding His Word in our hearts. When we do that we will not be swayed by every wind of doctrine but will stand steady before Him.

The last two verses promise us that God will work in our lives and in the life of our alcoholic loved one. "But the salvation of the righteous is of the Lord: he is their strength in the time of trouble. And the Lord shall help them . . . because they trust in him."

Lay hold of the promise by faith, and knowing God is at work will bring you peace in spite of the problem. It will lead you toward victory moment by moment and day by day.

We can reach this goal when we observe a regular time each morning for Bible study and prayer, taking the psalms as a special message from God to us. As God delivered David, so will He bring you through the dark days with a sweet spirit and a kindly attitude.

Many find help by joining Al-Anon, an organization of people who are not alcoholics but have an alcoholic in their immediate families. Here a person may be helped to overcome prejudices regarding the alcoholic that may cause obstacles to understanding and treating him successfully. Many families and friends refuse to recognize that the alcoholic is suffering from a very real problem of addiction he must be delivered from. The alcoholic himself often doesn't recognize his addiction. Understanding this, we should be more tolerant and play our family program in such a way that our alcoholic will voluntarily accept help.

We are told that only 15 percent of the alcoholics in this country seek help of their own free will. Most of the patients in the nearly four thousand alcohol treatment centers in the United States were admitted through intervention. We will go into that subject in detail in a later chapter.

Don't make the error of thinking of an alcoholic as a weak-willed person. His will may be warped, but he is not weak. He is as stubborn as an ox. When his will is brought into line with God's will, he will not only stop drinking but will remain sober.

A wife who wishes to remain anonymous wrote an AA pamphlet setting down some suggestions for the wife of an alcoholic to guide her treatment of him.

1. Never lose your temper. Even though your husband becomes unbearable and you have to leave him temporarily, do so without rancor. Patience and good temper are most necessary.
2. Never tell him what he must do about his drinking. If he gets the idea you are a nag or a killjoy, your chances of accomplishing anything useful will be zero. He will use that as an excuse to drink more. He will tell you that he is misunderstood. That may lead to lonely evenings for you. He may seek someone else to console him—and not always another man.
3. Be determined that your husband's drinking is not going to spoil your relationship with your children or your friends. They need your companionship and your help. It is possible to have a full and useful life, even though your husband continues to drink. We know women who are unafraid, even happy, under those conditions. Do not set your heart on reforming your husband. You may be unable to do so, no matter how hard you try.

Humanly speaking it is impossible for us to have a happy life under such circumstances. Yet we can have a victorious, happy Christian life if we put our trust in the Lord, have devotions regularly, and take an active part in the public worship of our church.

THE CHURCH'S ROLE

An ironic though tragic fact to be faced in the treatment of the alcoholic is that those who have the least to do with him are those who are best able to help him. So often, when an alcoholic is discovered in a congregation, the members react with condemnation, shunning him until he has "proved" himself. There are times when such condemnation spills over to engulf the individual's family as well.

The church's attitude toward the individual, the way in which they accept him in fellowship or reject him, can have much to do with whether he succeeds in the struggle for sobriety.

We saw that demonstrated very graphically in two youthful alcoholics in the same community. One was gathered up by the congregation of the church he attended. They lifted him into close communion and fellowship, and his Christian life blossomed. The other was tolerated by the church he chose to attend, but that was all. Though he had made a profession of faith in Christ, the congregation withheld themselves from him. The first of these young men was triumphantly victorious over alcohol addiction; the other failed miserably.

Our churches need to realize that they can perform a vital service for God and their communities by coming to grips with the problem of alcoholism. Alcoholics are all around us. If the churches become concerned and informed about the problem so they take an intelligent, realistic approach, they will soon find that local agencies dealing with the problem on the secular level will be anxious to have the assistance of the church.

It would be good for the pastor and as many lay workers as possible to attend seminars on the subject held by medical schools and psychiatric institutes and also to get acquainted with the men on the staffs of local rescue missions and become involved in their programs.

One of the ministries the Lord has opened for me has been seminars with the Christian approach to alcoholism. We have had the privilege of conducting these seminars all over the United States and Canada for the past nineteen years and have found them to be very successful.

Unfortunately it is difficult to get the pastors involved in such meetings. Laymen come out and so do the families of alcoholics, but many pastors feel they are too busy or that they don't need special help for dealing with the problem.

Surveys indicate that the first place the alcoholic will come for help is to the church pastor. And so often, the pastor is unable to read the signs and doesn't really understand the problem. For those reasons he turns the alcoholic off. No one knows how many opportunities are lost because the pastor failed to understand the needs of the person coming to him for help.

A good place for a local pastor to start in preparing himself to help treat alcoholics is to contact the International Service office of Alcoholics Victorious. They can acquaint him with literature that will be of help and will assist him if he feels the need to start an Alcohlics Victorious program in his church or community.

At least one of the more than four thousand secular alcoholic treatment centers should be within driving distance of most churches. It would be a help for the pastor to visit such a center and become acquainted with the director and the staff. I have known of pastors who have been able to influence a program that was not as spiritually oriented as they would like by quietly and wisely making friends with the people involved. If the pastor's spirit is cooperative and understanding, it is surprising how well he will be received among people who have a heart for reaching the homeless, helpless alcoholic.

There are also a number of fine Christian rehabilitation centers across the country. One that stands out to me is the Keswick Colony of Mercy in Whiting, New Jersey. They are probably the oldest Christian-oriented rehab program in the country and have an outstanding record of recovery for the people who are sent there.

Church libraries ought to have a section with books on the subject of alcohol and alcohol addiction. In addition to the books on the subject published by Christian publishers it would be wise to go over the list of books in a secular bookstore in order to get additional technical help. (Such books should be carefully screened by a knowledgeable individual before they are placed on the shelves, of course.) Such an assortment will provide the congregation with vital information on a perplexing subject and especially for those among the congregation who have an alcoholic in their families.

An alcohol addict who sees such books in the church library or mentioned from time to time in the bulletin will realize that the people in the church are concerned about individuals like him. He might find real help in the books, but even if he doesn't read them, the very fact that such books are in the church library can help to make the bond of friendship and fellowship with Christian people a bit stronger.

At the end of the book you will find a list of titles that will help you and the members of your church in understanding the problem better and in knowing how to deal with it. Don't forget to put the book you are now reading in your church library!

As we consider the church's role in helping the alcoholic, we must not forget that the average alcoholic feels uncomfortable when he first starts going to church. "They'd fall over in a faint if I went there," I have been told times without number.

And the first few times he will undoubtedly feel ill at ease. It is up to the members of the congregation to show the individual that he is not only welcome, but that they are *glad* he came.

A small central Nebraska church caught the vision of reaching such people. They weren't thinking solely of helping the alcoholic, but God used their efforts in that way. They were concerned about the number of parents who brought their children to Sunday school but didn't stay themselves. Efforts were made to get them into a Sunday school class, but without success. The pastor finally realized that although his congregation was friendly these parents felt strange in church.

So a class was organized to meet in his home during the Sunday school hour. Coffee was served, and the Bible was studied in an informal atmosphere. No effort was made to contact those with special problems, but of the fifteen enrolled during the first several months (the class divided in two to keep the groups small) it was discovered that three had definite drinking problems. Two of the three have been able to break their alcohol addiction by the power of the gospel of Jesus Christ. The third is still being worked with. He doesn't feel out of place in the group; he attends regularly and is honestly seeking help.

We might be able to assist the alcoholic by starting a class like this, or through some other means of showing the stranger that he is welcome with us. Warmth and fellowship can make the difference in whether or not we reach the alcoholic for Christ and thus meet his spiritual needs.

As we have said before, it matters not whether the person seeking to help the alcoholic is an ex-alcoholic or not. So long as the love of Christ burns in our hearts and we have compassion for those who are lost, we can be used of God.

Since dealing with the alcoholic requires so much time, the pastor with a burden for those who are slaves to alcohol would be wise to consider the organization of a team to help him. The team should be composed of men and women of unqualified dedication to the Lord, men and women of spiritual maturity who are willing to make very real sacrifices for the cause of Christ.

The pastor would also have to enlist families who would be willing to share their homes with strangers —who would be willing to spend any number of evenings with others whose homes and lives have been battered by the bruising forces of alcoholism. Associating with those who have been undergoing great trials and problems isn't always the most pleasant sort of companionship. And any results would have to be measured, necessarily, in months rather than hours. But a vital contribution can be made by Christians who are willing to make sacrifices.

In addition, the pastor should have a good medical doctor on his team, if one is available in his congregation. If not, he may be able to get the help of a physician in the community. Such a man would be most valuable in giving medical advice and assistance when necessary.

The very existence of such a team would be proof to the alcoholic that the church truly wanted to help him.

Although the alcoholic needs fellowship desperately, it is not always easy to get him to attend services at church right away. Often the alcoholic has a fear of people. This, in addition to shame for his actions, makes it hard for him to face an entire congregation. But a single member of the team could befriend him and provide him with fellowship by arranging to meet with him for Bible study and prayer (perhaps once a week).

I have seen this done. I know it works.

The team member and his wife could go a step further by making friends with the alcoholic's family. They could share God's love on a family basis. The alcoholic's wife or husband would then have a concerned Christian friend to whom she could turn for counsel and advice, and the alcoholic would begin to feel the dignity of being accepted as an individual. As the friendship develops, an attempt could be made to get the alcoholic's family into Sunday school and the fellowship of the church.

ALCOHOLICS ANONYMOUS AND ALCOHOLICS VICTORIOUS

The pastor and the church should cooperate with AA or Alcoholics Victorious, if the latter organization is available in the community.

AV has four steps in its year-long program of advancement. When the individual joins Alcoholics Victorious he receives a novice card and is a novice for three months. Then for another three months he becomes a pathfinder and in a ceremony is given a pathfinder's card. At the end of six months of abstinence he is given a victor's card, which he carries until he has been in the organization for a year. If he should slip and take a drink at any time during the year he has to start over as a novice. When he has abstained for a year he is given a crusader's card and pin.

Alcoholics Victorious has a short creed:

1. I realize that I cannot overcome the drink habit myself. I believe the power of Jesus Christ is available to help me. I believe that through acceptance of Him as my personal Savior I am a new man (2 Corinthians 5:17).

2. Because the presence of God is manifested through continued prayer, I will set aside two periods every day for communion with my heavenly Father. I realize my need for daily living (Psalm 24:1-5).

3. I recognize my need of Christian fellowship, and will therefore fellowship with Christians. I know that in order to be victorious, I must keep active in the service of Christ, and I will help others through my victory.

4. I do not partake of any beverage containing alcohol. I know that it is the first drink that does the harm. Therefore I do not drink. I will stay away from places where the temptation to drink might be, and from the companions who might tempt me. I can be victorious because I know that God's strength is sufficient to supply all my needs.

In various parts of the country people have started groups similar to AV but use other names. The Schicks in Des Moines, Iowa, are a good example. They were specialists in family counseling and formed what is known as the Gilead Ministry. It wasn't long until they realized that almost every family they were working with had the abuse of alcohol somewhere in the background.

They saw the need of a support group that would be helpful to the alcoholic and his family. Though they, like Garland Thompson, had never had an alcohol problem they founded Mountain Movers, an organization that has proved to be very effective.

David Garrison had gone to Viet Nam as a soldier and, though he was from a devout Christian family, was addicted to both alcohol and drugs. Somehow he got a copy of *God Is for the Alcoholic* and was helped so much by it he wanted to meet me. He outlined a plan for a program quite similar to the one the Schicks had developed in Des Moines. He named his group Stepping Stones. It is a biblically centered program and is very effective.

The First Assembly of God church in Tacoma, Washington, has started a group, The Taste of New Wine, using the last section of this book as the basis for their program. It too is accomplishing excellent results.

Alcoholics Anonymous had a spiritual beginning, though they feel that they can best serve as a secular organization. Their twelve steps are based on Christian principles.

1. *We admitted we were powerless over alcohol—that our lives had become unmanageable.* "For I know that in me (that is, in my flesh,) dwelleth no good thing: for to will is present with me; but how to perform that which is good I find not" (Romans 7:18).

2. *We came to believe that a power greater than ourselves could restore us to sanity.* "Let every soul be subject unto the higher powers. For there is no power but of God" (Romans 13:1).

3. *We made a decision to turn our will and our lives over to the care of God as we understood Him.* "Present your bodies a living sacrifice, holy, acceptable unto God, which is your reasonable service" (Romans 12:1).

4. *We made a searching and fearless moral inventory of ourselves.* "Let us search and try our ways, and turn again to the Lord" (Lamentations 3:40).

5. *We admitted to God, to ourselves, and to another human being the exact nature of our wrongs.* "Confess your faults one to another, and pray one for another, that ye may be healed" (James 5:16).

6. *We were entirely ready to have God remove all these defects of character.* "Humble yourselves in the sight of the Lord, and he shall lift you up" (James 4:10).

7. *We humbly asked Him to remove all our shortcomings.* "If we confess our sins, he is faithful and just to for-

give us our sins, and to cleanse us from all unrighteousness" (1 John 1:9).

8. *We made a list of all persons we have harmed and
became willing to make amends to them all.* "Therefore
all things whatsoever ye would that men should do to you,
do ye even so to them: for this is the law and the prophets"
(Matthew 7:12).

9. *We made direct amends to such people wherever
possible, except when to do so would injure them or others.* "Therefore if thou bring thy gift to the altar, and there
rememberest that thy brother hath ought against thee;
leave there thy gift. . . . First be reconciled to thy brother,
and then come and offer thy gift" (Matthew 5:23-24).

10. *We continued to take personal inventory and
when we were wrong, promptly admitted it.* "For I say,
through the grace given unto me, to every man that is
among you, not to think of himself more highly than he
ought to think; but to think soberly" (Romans 12:3).

11. *We sought through prayer and meditation to im-
prove our conscious contact with God as we understood
Him, praying only for knowledge of His will for us and the
power to carry that out.* "If any of you lack wisdom, let
him ask of God, that giveth to all men liberally, and upbraideth not; and it shall be given him" (James 1:5).

12. *Having had a spiritual experience as the result of
these steps, we tried to carry this message to alcoholics,
and practice these principles in all our affairs.* "Brethren, if
a man be overtaken in a fault, ye which are spiritual, restore such an one in the spirit of meekness; considering
thyself, lest thou also be tempted" (Galatians 6:1).

How can we help the alcoholic? By creating around
him an atmosphere that creates in him a desire for help.
One of the most effective ways of doing that is to offer him
fellowship in the name of our loving Lord, of whom it was
said, "God sent not his Son into the world to condemn the
world; but that the world through him might be saved"
(John 3:17).

ELEVEN
PLAN TO BE LONG-SUFFERING

Someone has said the patience of Job would have been sorely tried by an alcoholic. It may seem an exaggeration to some, but not to me or my family. I put my wife and children through that sort of tribulation. I didn't realize it then, as I do now.

"This is a faithful saying, and worthy of all acceptation, that Christ Jesus came into the world to save sinners; of whom I am chief. Howbeit for this cause I obtained mercy, that in me first Jesus Christ might shew forth all longsuffering, for a pattern to them which should hereafter believe on him to life everlasting" (1 Timothy 1:15-16).

Like Paul, I was a wicked sinner. Although it was years ago and I know that both God and my family have forgiven me, I am still unable to sleep when I get to thinking of the things I used to do that disgraced my family and hurt them so terribly.

But God saved me and delivered me and my family.

He can do the same for any individual—even the degenerate, filthy alcohol addict—who calls upon His name. Christ shows His long-suffering to us as a pattern for others to follow in their treatment of sinners. No one needs that pattern more than the one with an alcoholic in the family. We must have the assurance in our hearts that God is not only interested in our alcoholic but loves him and wants to help him. We also must be aware of our own relationship to God and the problems He had in bringing us to the place where we could be used of Him.

He knows all about us—our heartaches and trials, our disappointments and our deepest desires. And in His Word He gives us hope and encouragement. "But thou, O Lord, art a God full of compassion, and gracious, longsuffering, and plenteous in mercy and truth" (Psalm 86:15).

Patience and the ability to suffer long are character traits that are not easily attained. We must ask God to make us patient and long-suffering as we deal with our alcoholic. This applies to everyone who is involved in working with him—members of the immediate family, the pastor or counselor, or concerned friends. We must trust God and believe that He is working regardless of what we see, hear, or feel. Unwavering confidence and trust in God are imperative if we are to accomplish our goal in working with our alcoholic.

STEPS OF INTERVENTION

If he is still drinking, we must bring our loved one to the place where he (or she) will request help to overcome his drinking problem.

It has been said that nothing can be done for alcoholics until they are ready and willing to accept help. In many ways that is true. Yet alcoholic treatment centers have found that there is much that can be done to bring alcoholics to the place where they recognize that they must have help.

Intervention into the life of the alcoholic by society, business, and the family can bring the addict to the place where he will accept help. Intervention is a biblical principle.

"If your brother sins against you, go and show him his fault, just between the two of you. If he listens to you, you have won your brother over. But if he will not listen, take one or two others along, so that 'every matter may be established by the testimony of two or three witnesses.' If he refuses to listen to them, tell it to the church; and if he refuses to listen even to the church, treat him as you would a pagan or a tax collector" (Matthew 18:15-17, NIV).

Our alcoholic loved one, either male or female, has sinned against us by lying, cheating, and stealing. He has sinned against us in the things he has said to us and about us and often in the physical abuse he has forced upon us in his drunkenness. We are directed to go to the alcoholic when he is sober and talk with him about it.

It is our responsibility to tell him how he is hurting us and the family—how he is jeopardizing his job and his own health. In a kind, loving way we should try to encourage him to take some sort of treatment. It may be getting him to attend a group program like AA or AV.

But if he refuses we need to take the next step, that of intervening. We must show him just how he has hurt those who love him and how much he needs to come to a place of deliverance. We must try to get him to recognize that he needs treatment.

Since alcoholism is a sin sickness that begins in the state of drunkenness and ends in real physical illness, we need to try to implement treatment as quickly as possible. To do so will mean less destruction to the alcoholic and his physical and mental health. It also will produce a greater likelihood of recovery.

If he will not listen when we talk to him we must go on to the next step; take one or two others along so every matter will have been established by the testimony of witnesses. There is a certain group of people who are most effective in the intervention process—the wife or husband of the alcoholic, the children, close friends, business associates or the employer, the pastor, and a trained intervention counselor.

A program must be worked out, establishing in every detail the items we want to talk to the alcoholic about. It accomplishes very little to speak in general terms. "I think you drink too much," or, "Your actions are hurting me and the children." We must be specific.

Something like this drives the problem home. "Mom, do you remember when you were going to drive my girl friend and me to camp? You had been drinking, and we were scared of the way you drove. We were afraid you would hit another car and kill us all. You finally had to pull off to the side of the road and sleep it off. I was so ashamed of what happened that I never wanted to see Susan again."

"Dad, do you remember that weekend we planned to go fishing, but you got so drunk you couldn't even get into the boat? It spoiled the weekend for all of us."

"Honey, do you remember when I planned to take you out for an anniversary dinner? We were going to have a great time. I bought you that diamond ring you always wanted because our business was finally good enough that I felt I could afford it. But when I got home with the ring you were in the bedroom drunk. You weren't dressed, and the whole anniversary was washed out. I just want you to know that I still have the ring. I would like to give it to you once you get your life straightened out."

You will note that these examples call to mind specific incidents that are certain to draw reactions on the part of the alcoholic. He may rebel, deny it, or fight back, but if you have gone over it carefully in your mind, if you take every matter and establish it so your testimony is true and straight and honest, the chances are good that the alcoholic who is confronted in this way will eventually accept treatment.

The employer or a business associate can play an important part in the matter of intervention.

Stan is a good example. He had worked at his job for a number of years, but his drinking reached the point where something had to be done. He was coming to work with such hangovers that he couldn't adequately handle his job. The supervisor called him and his wife in and told him he was fired because of poor performance brought on by his drinking. If he would go through a treatment program at a nearby center, however, he could come back to work. He didn't like the idea, but faced with that choice, he went. At this writing it has been two years since he returned, and he is still sober.

The employer has a big investment in the alcoholic employee. It is often cheaper for him to go through the inconvenience of sending an alcoholic to treatment than it is to fire him and train somebody else to take over the job.

When the employer is brought in, he does not talk about the individual's drinking. He talks about how it affects his performance on the job or the effect his drinking has on the customers he contacts. Of course the trained intervention counselor is careful to keep everything on track. He will also have told the family what they can expect and will have advised them concerning the treatment facilities that are nearby. Then he tries to help the alcoholic select a good treatment center.

The pastor also can play a very important part. He might not be in the confrontation team. It is usually better to have people in that role who can bring pressure of sorts to bear. Yet he can be an encouraging factor. He can carefully set the family up in prayer and minister to them in a loving way, assuring them that God is interested in them and their alcoholic and that He wants to restore him to sobriety and to his rightful place in the family unit, the church, and the community.

This method of intervention may seem too simplistic to be effective, but I can assure you that every time I have followed the admonishment of Matthew 18:15-17 I have had successful results. Some of the experiences were trying at first, but they worked out in a satisfactory way.

The key to intervention is love. Some psychologists call it "tough love." That is the kind of love God has—the kind of love that says, "I can't look on sin, but I so love my creation that I sent my only begotten Son that whosoever believeth in Him shall not perish but have everlasting life" (see John 3). God gave up His very Son that you and I might have life. And Christ gave up His life that you and I might live.

We must love so much that we are willing to give ourselves up so that someone else might live. That means we have to call a spade a spade, just as our Lord did. "All have sinned and come short of the glory of God" (Romans 3:23). "There is none righteous, no, not one" (Romans 3:10). "The wages of sin is death; but the gift of God is eternal life through Jesus Christ our Lord" (Romans 6:23).

We must never try to intervene if we have bitterness in our hearts or if we have an unforgiving spirit. We must get those things straightened out with God and our fellowman before we try intervention.

It has been estimated that 50 percent of the alcoholics today are women. Alcohol affects women differently during the days immediately prior to menstruation than during the remainder of the month. Women taking oral contraceptives metabolize alcohol more slowly than those not on the pill. That means they probably become intoxicated faster and remain drunk longer.

Studies indicate that women alcoholics have a greater vulnerability to liver disease than men. They also may run a higher risk of pneumonia. And, interestingly enough, a woman alcoholic will usually pinpoint specific distressing situations as the cause of her alcoholism, whereas men don't.

Women will often say they started drinking because of the death of a loved one, a divorce, grown children leaving home, obstetrical or gynecological problems, breast cancer, and even the menstrual cycle. These things all deeply affect women, and they find that drinking helps them escape some of the pain.

I remember the day a Cadillac screeched to a halt in front of our office at the mission in Omaha. A distressed-looking woman got out and barged into my office.

"I did it again, Pastor Jerry! I did it again!"

I had never seen her before, but at that time I had a Sunday morning TV program and she knew I worked with alcoholics. Finally I got her quieted and said, "Now, tell me, what did you do again?"

"I forgot to pick up my five-year-old when he got out of kindergarten this noon!"

"Tell me about it."

Things had gone well with her as long as her husband held a minor position at work, but as he advanced in his company she felt that she was being left behind—that she was inadequate. She didn't think she was up to the social life that was required of her now that he was a prominent businessman in the community. She started drinking in a effort to escape and became addicted to the point where she was blacking out and couldn't even remember to pick up their little boy at school.

Another woman had a different problem. She was a Christian woman and seemed to be making progress in our counseling sessions. She was attending church regularly and had even persuaded her husband to go with her. Then I got a call saying she had fallen again and would I be willing to counsel with her once more.

"Why did you go back?" I asked her. "God had given you a new life. He had made you a new creature. You are a member of His family. Why did you embarrass Him and your family and our friends by going back to beverage alcohol?"

"I just couldn't stop sinning. I kept sinning and couldn't stop it."

"What did you do that was so sinful that you couldn't confess it and allow the Lord to forgive you?"

She didn't want to tell me but was so desperate that she did. "I have sexual relations with my husband. And now that I am saved, that—that is sinful."

This dear woman had been taught that sex, even within the confines of marriage, was sin. As long as she was not saved it was all right for them to have sex, but once she became a Christian it was sin.

We taught her what the Bible has to say about the marriage bed being undefiled and that the union of the husband and wife is an example of Christ and His church, that sex is only sin when committed outside of marriage.

She experienced great release and found complete victory in her life. She is still walking with the Lord today, a great testimony to His saving grace. Like most women she was very sensitive and needed to be taught God's Word.

Men also need to be taught their self-worth, but it seems more important that women understand their importance to God, to their husbands, and to their families. They can then see that they no longer need the crutch of beverage alcohol to make life palatable. They can say no to that afternoon cocktail and begin to enjoy the Lord, their families, and living.

We must be ever mindful that our confidence and trust is in God if we are to be successful in bringing our alcoholic loved one back to sobriety. We must believe that it is His desire to free our alcoholic from the bonds of addiction and give him a new life. We will only be disappointed and heartbroken if we do not look beyond what we see in the individual we have been working with, to God, who will give us the strength and patience we need during this very trying period.

"My brethren, count it all joy when ye fall into divers temptations; knowing this, that the trying of your faith worketh patience. But let patience have her perfect work, that ye may be perfect and entire, wanting nothing" (James 1:2-4).

Not long ago a Texan wrote of the simple faith and courage and patience of his wife during the years he was a slave to alcohol. "She refused to let me break up our home," he said, "and she refused to lose faith that one day God would deliver me from alcohol addiction."

This woman put up with a drunkard husband for fifteen years, her faith never wavering, before God brought her husband to a saving knowledge of the Lord Jesus Christ and set him free from alcoholism. In her loneliness, despite all the bad reports that came to her about him, she stood strong and unmovable in her faith. With patience and long-suffering she waited until God answered her prayers. Just so, He will answer your prayers if you continue to trust

Him and do not grow weary of waiting.

LESSONS FROM THE PRODIGAL SON

In ministering to the alcoholic, we can find help for such ministry by reading the story of the prodigal son found in Luke 15.

Headstrong and wayward, the prodigal demanded all his inheritance so he could leave home and do as he pleased without interference from anyone. Knowing there was nothing he would be able to do or say that would change the young man's mind, his father let him go.

The same mulish determination to go his own way is seen in our alcoholic. He is going to do as he pleases and when he pleases. All of the arguments we throw at him and all the nagging we do isn't going to stop his drinking at this point.

The prodigal spent his inheritance in a long orgy, during which he gave not one thought to his parents or the anguish he was causing them. His money did not last indefinitely, however. The day came when he was broke and hungry enough to take the most lowly of jobs, that of herding pigs, in order to get something to eat.

Then something happened.

He got to thinking about the home where he had been raised. Even his father's servants received better treatment than he was now getting. He saw the folly of his life of sin. He saw that he was spiritually and morally bankrupt. He had reached absolute bottom.

In the same way the alcoholic wakes up to his own particular pigsty—in a rescue mission, a city jail where he has spent the night after being picked up for intoxication, or perhaps in a hotel room or seated on the edge of his bed at home. But the location is not so important as his coming face to face with himself. He knows that he cannot go on the way he has been. He begins to compare what he could have with what he now has. His heart starts to burn within him.

The prodigal decided to go home. He went penitently, asking nothing.

When the alcoholic reaches the place where he honestly admits that he has a problem and wants help, something can be done for him. That is why it is so important for his family to keep their home life operating as near normally as possible. The atmosphere of the home should be such that it will encourage the alcoholic to want to be a normal member of the family once more.

LESSONS FROM THE PRODIGAL'S FATHER

The father of the prodigal kept the home atmosphere as it was, and when the wayward son returned, he was brought into this home and helped.

Aside from having a well-run home for the prodigal to return to, the father expected an answer to his prayers. He was watching for his boy's return. "But when he was yet a great way off, his father saw him, and had compassion, and ran, and fell on his neck, and kissed him" (Luke 15:20).

That is the attitude we must have. After praying, we must expect God to do something to answer our prayers.

When the son got home, his father let him resume his position in the family. In the case of the alcoholic that may not be as simple as it would seem. Many serious problems can arise when the alcoholic is received back into the family. Many times a wife is bitterly disappointed when she discovers that she cannot turn the clock back to the way things were before when they were first married. We must start with the situation at hand, which means forgiving and forgetting. Forgiving may seem easy. The forgetting is much more difficult. Remember, we have never forgiven if we haven't forgotten.

Recovery must start when an alcoholic comes home, honestly wanting to quit drinking. Of course, his own will-power is not enough. He must have Christ as his Savior so that he has a strong spiritual basis upon which to build. We must build upon this foundation together, growing spiritually and closer to one another.

It may not be easy for us to have in our hearts the joy the prodigal's father had as his son came home. He said, "This my son was dead, and is alive again; he was lost, and is found. And they began to be merry" (Luke 15:24).

A merry, joyful, happy heart will go a long way in helping your alcoholic make a successful recovery. But such joy can be ours only as a fruit of the Holy Spirit (Galatians 5:22-23).

LESSONS FROM THE PRODIGAL'S BROTHER

The prodigal's father was overjoyed that his wayward son was home once more, but the elder son in the family was not at all happy about it. He had stayed home and worked while his younger brother was squandering his share of the family inheritance. He had seen the hurt in his parents' faces and had been touched with jealousy as he saw how they watched the road for signs of the prodigal's return. Now that he was back, the elder brother's jealousy became a consuming fire.

Although we may not be aware of it, each of us has something of the elder brother's attitude. But if we are going to have the patience and long-suffering needed to help our alcoholic, we are going to have to protect ourselves, and him, from the angry jealousy that will flare every time we think things aren't going exactly as we feel they should.

We have been praying earnestly for the deliverance of our alcoholic from the power of beverage alcohol. We have seen him make a profession of taking Christ as his Savior and have been happier about that than about anything else in the world. Yet the hurts and heartaches we have suffered are still very personal and real.

We have seen our children suffer, often because of the financial situation our alcoholic's drinking has created. And we see their personalities change. If we aren't very careful and aren't living close to God, we will build such a spirit of resentment that we will explode when things aren't going the way we think they should.

What in the attitude of the elder brother are we going to have to guard against?

First, we will have to guard against jealousy.

On one occasion I mentioned this to a person with whom I was counseling. She was very much disturbed.

"What do you mean, jealousy?" she bristled. "I've been longing and praying for years that my husband would be set free from the hold liquor has on him. Who can say that I could ever be jealous of him if that should happen?"

I told her about a woman who was exactly in the same position and how jealous she got without even realizing it. She was jealous of her place in the hearts and lives of her children. During the years her husband was drinking so heavily, the children came to her for advice and counsel. She enforced discipline and was the focal point in their lives.

Suddenly her husband was sober. He took an interest in the children, and they began to come to him with decisions instead of to their mother. As he assumed his rightful position in the family, she was filled with resentment and became irritable, angry, and very jealous. Her jealousy almost caused her husband to lose his battle with alcohol. Fortunately, she was wise enough to see what had happened to her, once it was pointed out, and she did something about it.

Even having our alcoholic accepted back into the community can create jealousy that Satan can use as a barb against him. If he is making a successful comeback, he wants to tell somebody about it and often gets extra recognition. He may get involved in church activities, or in making his twelve-step calls for Alcoholics Anonymous, or in his responsibilities in Alcoholics Victorious. It is easy for us to feel neglected and jealous if those things seem to take too much of his time or attention.

"I used to be a 'bottle widow,'" one lovely Christian wife told me. "Now I'd have to say I'm some other kind of a widow. My husband is always going somewhere to give his testimony or to witness."

In her case she was mature enough to understand and accept the situation.

The second trait of the elder son that we must guard against is self-pity.

"Lo, these many years do I serve thee, neither transgressed I at any time thy commandment: and yet thou never gavest me a kid, that I might make merry with my friends" (Luke 15:29).

Self-pity is apt to rear its ugly head and blight our lives if we don't recognize it and pray for victory over it.

Many alcohol addicts have staggering financial problems. Their wives have had to work to support the family and to maintain some kind of economic stability. Suppose, in a situation such as this, the alcoholic makes a financial investment without mentioning it to his wife and loses all the money—money that is so desperately needed. There is a very real danger in such a case that the wife might feel so abused and resentful, even though she says little, that her husband might be driven back to drinking again.

Or take the husband of an alcoholic wife. She has been making good progress. The routine of the home is almost back to normal. Rejoicing that they are approaching a normal life, the husband asks his boss home to dinner.

The wife doesn't drink, but she is so nervous and upset that she can't manage everything. The meat is burned, and the dinner is a miserable failure. I've heard husbands in such situations air their feelings bitterly.

"I've put up with this for years," they say. "But even when she's sober, she isn't a good housekeeper."

To keep from pitying ourselves and allowing self-pity to destroy the progress that has been made, we must patiently wait upon the Lord and show long-suffering to the alcoholic.

The third fault of the elder brother is the way he constantly remembered the past. He forgave nothing and forgot nothing. He held against his younger brother everything that had happened. "But as soon as this thy son was come, which hath devoured thy living with harlots, thou hast killed for him the fatted calf" (Luke 15:30).

We too find it difficult to put away all that has happened in the past. We profess to forget, but we don't, really. We keep looking at our alcoholic and at everything he does.

"That's just the way he used to do before he went on a drunk," we say, fearfully measuring every action.

If we are going to help our alcoholic, what shall we do with our memories of the way things used to be? We've got to face things as they are now and build solidly from the point where we now stand.

In spite of the danger of becoming like the elder brother, there is a way of victory. The prodigal's father showed his elder son the way. He said to him, "It was meet that we should make merry, and be glad: for this thy brother was dead, and is alive again; and was lost, and is found" (Luke 15:32).

We must constantly remind ourselves that our alcoholic is like the prodigal son. Once he was lost, now he is found. Once he was dead, now he lives. If we want to be successful in helping our alcohol addict along the road to recovery, we must combine praise for good things with our long-suffering and patience. You can be long-suffering and patient if you have the confidence and trust expressed by the psalmist David when he wrote:

> In thee, O Lord, do I put my trust: . . . For thou art my rock and my fortress: therefore for thy name's sake lead me, and guide me. . . . Into thine hand I commit my spirit: thou hast redeemed me, O Lord God of truth. . . . Oh how great is thy goodness, which thou hast laid up for them that fear thee; which thou hast wrought for them that trust in thee before the sons of men! Thou shalt hide them in the secret of thy presence from the pride of man: thou shalt keep them secretly in a pavilion from the strife of tongues. . . . Be of good courage, and he shall strengthen your heart, all ye that hope in the Lord." (Psalm 31:1, 3, 5, 19-20, 24)

TWELVE
PRACTICE FIRMNESS

Somewhere, somehow, many of us have got the misconceived idea that there is no rebuke in God's love; that it is sickeningly sweet and forgiving, even to those who are unrepentant and whose sin is unconfessed. We sometimes seem to believe that God loves so much He would never punish anyone. That is not true.

God loves us so much He will not allow us to name Christ as Savior and continue in our old sin without severely chastising us to bring us back to Him.

LET THE ALCOHOLIC STAND ON HIS OWN TWO FEET

Christ gave explicit instructions to the disciples about how they should act in the face of sin and wrongdoing. "Take heed to yourselves: If thy brother trespass against thee, rebuke him; and if he repent, forgive him. And if he trespass against thee seven times in a day, and seven times in a day turn again to thee, saying, I repent; thou shalt forgive him" (Luke 17:3-4).

If we sin, we should be rebuked. If we repent, we ought to be forgiven. This is the way Christ says we should be with one another. God does the same in His relationships with us. Because He loves us He cannot allow us to sin without rebuking us. "Rebuke a wise man, and he will love thee" (Proverbs 9:8).

"Let the righteous smite me; it shall be a kindness: and let him reprove me; it shall be an excellent oil, which shall not break my head: for yet my prayer also shall be in their calamities" (Psalm 141:5).

When we deal with the alcohol addict, we need to rebuke him, for in his downward progression into alcoholism he has developed three characteristics:

1. He has become a crafty liar.
2. He seeks someone to lean upon and becomes a very dependent individual.
3. He thinks only of himself and much prefers to be alone. His personality becomes egocentric and antisocial.

If our alcoholic is going to be helped, not only must his addiction to alcohol be broken, but his very personality must be redeveloped as well. If our alcoholic lies to us, we should quietly but firmly let him know that we are aware he is lying. The sooner he comes to the place where he has to face the truth, the sooner he is going to be set free from his warped personality and his addiction to alcohol.

The pamphlet *Trial and Error*, published by the Alcohol and Drug Addiction Research Foundation of Ontario, Canada, says this in its instructions for those with an alcoholic in the family: "The average alcoholic would not be able to function as long as he does if his wife or mother would allow him to stand on his own two feet where he properly belongs. Let him accept responsibility for his own actions. Allow him to retain his self-respect instead of slowly helping him to destroy himself."

The youngest son in a family I know was protected at every turn by his misguided Christian mother. Let John get in trouble with the law and she was there with her meager savings to get him out. When he served time for writing bad checks she bombarded the governor's office and the parole board with letters pleading for his release. When he was broke and needed a place of refuge he could always come home, regardless of the circumstances. She could never accept the fact that he was an alcoholic. In her eyes his difficulties were always caused by someone else. He died a few years ago in a flophouse in Cheyenne, Wyoming's skid row. Quite possibly, he could have been redeemed had she forced him to stand up or fall on his own. Her protection of him helped to keep him in the condition that broke her heart.

MAKE GROUND RULES

It is not wise to threaten the alcoholic. Neither is it a good practice to try to extract promises from him. But if our alcoholic should voluntarily make a promise when he is sober, he should be held to his agreement.

A couple who faced this situation came to me some time ago and asked me to marry them. Although they were both in their fifties, neither had been married before. Moreover, the man was an alcohol addict who had been dry for only six months. I knew him well, since I had been counseling with him for three years.

"Sally has wanted to marry you for five years," I reminded him, "but she has refused because of your drinking. If you are going to get married there has to be an agreement that you are not going to drink."

He nodded readily.

"If you take so much as a thimbleful of liquor, you should be put out of the house."

Both agreed that this was the only basis upon which they could have a happy marriage.

They had been married nine months when Tom took a glass of wine.

Tearfully she talked to me on the phone. "What should I do now?"

"You know what the agreement was."

She packed his clothes and put him out of the house. "When you're through drinking and ready to live a sober life again, you can come back," she told him.

She threw him out of the house ten different times in two-and-a-half years before he finally yielded to the Lord.

"I was lying on a hospital bed alone," he said, "when I realized that there was only one way I could be free. So I said, 'God, You take my life.' "

Today he has been completely delivered from addiction, and there is joy in that home because a wife stood firm. It wasn't easy for her. We spent a great deal of time counseling her and helping her through those difficult periods. But the result was victory through Christ. You too can have such a victory if you remain firm.

Protect Your Interests

Rev. Joseph Kellerman, director of the Charlotte, North Carolina, Council on Alcoholism at the time *God Is for the Alcoholic* was originally written, gives another warning. "Don't let the alcoholic outsmart you, for this teaches him to avoid responsibility and lose respect for you at the same time. Don't let the alcoholic exploit you or take advantage of you, for in so doing you'll become an accomplice in the evasion of responsibility."

I will never forget a couple that came to me with this sort of problem. The wife had a sizable bank account at the time they were married. Her husband insisted that she transfer her assets to a joint account, which she refused to do. When they came to me in a normal marriage counseling session to talk about the matter, it soon was brought out that he had a serious drinking problem. She had thought he would quit when they were married, but he hadn't.

As the session went on, it was apparent that he had insisted on seeing a counselor because he hoped he would find someone who would agree with him that her money should be in a joint account.

"You know," I said to him, privately, "I'm talking to you as one old drunk to another. When I was drinking I used to do anything and everything I could to outsmart my employers and my wife in order to get more time and more money for liquor. Are you sure this isn't why you want your wife's money in a joint account?''

He admitted that it was, and we were able to help him see his responsibility and to assume it.

MEAN WHAT YOU SAY

It is not wise to make threats to our alcoholic, but if we do, we must make sure that we're prepared to carry them out.

The woman who said she had threatened to leave her husband a hundred times for his drinking finally did so. It wasn't long until he was seeking help so he could get her back.

At the mission we made no threats to the men in our rehabilitation program, but we had some very definite regulations. The men knew when they came into our program voluntarily that if they had so much as a single beer, they would be removed from the program. If they wanted to come back, they would have to start at the bottom again and work their way up.

Usually the men had trouble in the second month of the program. That was when they were permitted to go out and work several days a week and keep the money. If they took a drink, we made them pack their clothes and leave. Some came back and tried again. The second time they were usually successful.

What worked with the men at the mission would work with our alcoholic. We must be firm and mean what we say.

DON'T DO FOR HIM WHAT HE SHOULD DO FOR HIMSELF

Women often have to go to work to support themselves and their children because of the alcohol addiction of their husbands. Out of necessity they begin to assume the full responsibility of the home and require nothing of their husbands in return.

It isn't easy for an alcoholic to get a job or hold one. He has probably spent a long period of time drifting from one place to another or not working at all. He has forgotten what it is like to have to work every day. However, he should be willing to assume some responsibility for the support and upkeep of his home.

In his moments of sobriety share with him the needs of the home, not as a nagging wife but as a loving wife who still believes that the husband is the head of the house. Impress upon him that he should share and give advice in those areas of responsibility.

When he starts working again, don't hold onto your job for reasons of security—because you feel he might have a relapse. If you feel you must keep your job, arrange to live on his salary. Discuss the matter with him and reach an agreement so he will never get the idea that he can fall back on you to take care of things. Work things out so he will always feel his responsibilities.

There is a very good chance, if this dependence is not broken, that he might go back to drinking again.

One of the benefits of presenting the gospel to the alcohol addict is that his faith in God will enable him to transfer his dependency from an individual or a group to God. God is the only one who can really help him and supply the strength and wisdom he needs in order to assume his responsibility. When an individual begins to assume responsibility, it isn't long until he begins to regain his self-respect. Another benefit from his faith in God is that his faith removes the tendency toward self-destruction, a tendency that is common to the alcoholic.

ASK ADVICE

Those who deal with a known alcoholic should always get advice from outside sources when a problem arises within the family. For instance, some time ago, a lovely Christian mother whose heart was being broken by the drinking of her alcoholic son called us for advice. Her son had been a very successful stock broker. Few people aside from his business partners, his closest friends, and his family—a prominent family in our city—even knew that he had a drinking problem. His partners in the broker-age firm kept him on at full salary for a number of years. Finally, when the situation got so bad they could no longer put up with it, they relieved him of all responsibility but placed him on a pension. His wife drank herself to death, and he seemed bent on doing the same thing.

It was at this point that his mother took him into her home. She was financially independent, but an unmarried daughter lived with her. The daughter had a job, contribut-ed to the upkeep of the home, and gave her mother the fellowship and companionship she needed. When the son moved in, nothing was said to him about his responsibili-ties. He moved into a room and proceeded to drink as much as before. The only thing that changed was the loca-tion.

When the situation became more than the two wom-en could bear, they called me. When I arrived at their home, I found that he had been in a drunken stupor for days. We got him to the hospital where he was dried out and released.

I tried talking with him, but he wouldn't listen.

When I talked with his mother and sister, I explained that he should have to pay his way, make some contribu-tion to the expenses of the family, and participate in the family life and fellowship—that he should not just stay in his room. I tried to make them see that he had to break his dependency.

They didn't accept my advice. They didn't understand the problem, and they thought the requirements I set down were too hard, not loving enough.

It wasn't long until I was called once more and asked to get him to the hospital. "No," I told them, "I'll not take him to the hospital this time. I suggest that you make a committal and have the authorities place him in the psy-chiatric ward of the county hospital."

They didn't think that was very kind, either, but in desperation they did it.

The shock of having a deputy sheriff take him to the county hospital was just what he needed to wake him up to the fact that he had a problem and had to have help. When he got home, he was ready for guidance. Some ground rules were laid down as to his responsibilities toward his family. He assumed them and today is a help to his mother rather than a liability. It all came about because she sought advice and followed it.

Actions Speak Louder than Words

In working with an alcoholic we must always go by what he does—not by what he says he is going to do. We should pay attention to what he says so we can help him hold to it, but we have to watch his actions to be sure he is living up to what he says.

I have often talked to men who start drinking again after having been dry for as long as a year or more. Usually they are horrified to find that they have again plummeted to the very depths of drunkenness.

I always go to great lengths to explain to them once more this terrible problem of addiction. This is something about which we must constantly remind our alcoholic, since many such people have an idea that they are going to make a successful recovery from alcoholism and then go back to drinking socially once more. We must always direct our activities with our alcoholic in such a way that we do not encourage social drinking.

A few years ago a study indicated that it was possible for an alcoholic to go back to social drinking after breaking the bonds of alcohol addiction. Studies before and since, however, have completely blasted that theory. A recovered alcoholic can never drink again, socially or in any other way, without plunging back into the abyss of alcohol addiction.

Often when I am talking with a man who has started

to drink once more after having been sober for a period, he will express bewilderment at what happened. "I can't understand it," he will say. "I want my family back worse than anything else in the world."

Sometimes an alcoholic can't understand why his family won't take him back immediately, and then we must point out to him the areas where he is failing. For example, he must understand that just the matter of going back to drink is something that is going to retard the reconciliation for from three to six months—and possibly for an entire year. No wife in her right mind is going to want to go back into the same old routine that caused all the trouble.

Then too it might be that he hasn't been doing anything constructive in trying to redeem his family. Perhaps he isn't making any contribution to their upkeep other than what has been required of him by a court order. He may not make an effort to find out how he can help his wife and children over and above this requirement in assuming his responsibilities as a husband and father.

He may say he wants his family back, but he gives the lie to what he says by making no effort to do those things he knows would show his wife that he is a different person.

One fellow I dealt with would take his children to Sunday school but would not go to church himself. He claimed to be making a recovery from alcohol addiction. He attended AA meetings once a week and claimed he was getting the spiritual backing he needed from those meetings. Yet his wife didn't see him going to church, and she knew that his habits hadn't changed. He might not have been drinking, but he was still hanging around the same old haunts with the same old friends.

He talked about being different, but his actions revealed that he was the same fellow he had always been. The only difference was that he hadn't had a drink. That didn't keep his wife from thinking that he was going to start drinking again at any time. And when he did fall over the line into another bout of drunkenness, she was certain that there was no hope for him. To my knowledge they never did get back together.

There are things we need to watch intelligently in our alcoholic. We need to be certain that his actions are where his desires and his talk are. When his actions change, we can be quite certain that he has changed as well.

Every once in a while we have come across some refreshing experiences that let us know it is all worthwhile. One such occasion when my wife and I traveled some distance from home to speak to an AA group, we met a local politician who had not been married long, although both he and his wife were in their late fifties.

My wife learned, as she talked with the wife, the reason for their late marriage. "We went together for sixteen years," she said, "but I wouldn't marry him because of his drinking problem. When he was delivered from his addiction by the power of God, I agreed to marry him. That was five years ago."

That is the sort of firmness we must have in dealing with an alcoholic.

I came across the opposite situation in dealing with another couple. The wife talked as though she wanted her husband free from addiction, but I noticed that she seemed to get enjoyment from the fact that he was an alcoholic. One day as I was seated in their home, I learned what the problem was. "I can't understand why Joe is like he is," she said. "I try to be kind and considerate to him. I even bring him breakfast in bed every morning." She didn't really want a husband. She wanted someone she could mother.

In later counseling sessions I began to point out to her that she wasn't really interested in seeing her husband escape his addiction, that she was interested only in taking care of him. We helped her see that God's plan is for the husband to be the head of the wife and as a father exercise authority over his children.

She saw that what I said was true and was able to face up to her attitude and come to the place where she was willing to change by the power of God. Then she was able to make a real contribution to our efforts to help her husband make a successful recovery.

BREAKING COMMUNITY DEPENDENCE

We have already mentioned the problem of the alcoholic's becoming dependent upon the community. Every city and town in America faces this problem.

For example, one city with which I am familiar is spending two million dollars a year in an attempt to cure 285 individuals of alcohol addiction. A look at the case histories of these men will reveal the startling fact that most of them rotate from one institution to another, year after year, without being helped. They depend upon community institutions for their survival and for aid and support.

At the missions we have been associated with we tried continually to break the alcoholic's dependence on the community. It is not easy. It requires close community cooperation to make any progress in breaking that dependence.

In dealing with this matter on a community level we have found that we have to deal with three types of alcohol addicts.

1. The *institutionalized alcoholic* has lived in an institution most of his life. He may have worked on the railroad or in construction crews where he has lived in dormitories and eaten in cafeterias or chow lines. Perhaps he has spent long periods in some jail or penitentiary or, because of his addiction, in a hospital for the treatment of alcoholism. At any rate, he becomes so accustomed to the care and routine of an institution that it is difficult for him to live outside such an atmosphere. When he is forced to be on his own and make decisions for himself he goes back to drink.

We need to recognize this man's problem and help him regain his self-respect. Working toward this end, we must furnish him with the right kind of atmosphere in which to live. He needs a home in a county institution (not a jail or mental hospital) where he can receive board and room, laundry, and a small salary. He could be used to clean public buildings or to care for the lawns and parks that belong to the city or county. His work should be the kind that will make a contribution to society. Providing him with a social situation like this will help him to overcome his alcohol addiction, and he will be paying his own way, thus saving the community and taxpayers the expense of taking care of him.

2. *Probationary alcoholics* are by far the largest group of alcoholics and are men who will need many counseling sessions. Some will require hospitalization to help them make a recovery, but they will need more than hospitalization to be successfully rehabilitated. After they have been dried out, someone is going to have to work with them for a long while, guiding and counseling them.

Most of these men could be productive. They are skilled or semiskilled laborers and could assume the responsibility of taking care of their families, who may be on some kind of government relief.

It seems to me that a program should be worked out that would permit such individuals to live in the institutions to which they are committed (people of this type usually come into our institutions through the courts because of drunkenness) and spend their nights there, but days could be spent working on normal jobs. Their wages could be sent to the family for support so they could be removed from the relief rolls.

That would do two things. First, it would help break the dependency of this individual on the community for the support of his family. Second, not many would care to continue in an arrangement where they had to spend their time in an institution and still had to work to support their families. My experience with the treatment of alcoholics leads me to the conviction that it wouldn't be long until such men would be looking for some type of program to help them get over their addiction.

Although a program of this type would have some legal complications, they should not be insurmountable.

Most alcoholics are good workmen, and it should not be difficult to induce employers to cooperate with such a program. A program like this would also give an opportunity for cooperation among the community, the employer, and the family in an effort to help this man to overcome his problem and to return to society as a useful citizen.

3. The *rehabilitated alcoholic* is the individual who came for help, went through the program of rehabilitation, received what was offered to him gratefully, and has put it to use. He is restored to his family and is finding his place in his church and the community.

What a joy to see such results in an individual who is an alcoholic!

THIRTEEN
HELPING THE TEENAGER

WHERE DO THEY LEARN IT?

There are a number of things we must remember in considering the problem of teenage drinking. Some aren't pleasant because they strike close to home. The young person sees every drink consumed by an adult he loves as a vote of approval for him to do the same.

The March 1983 issue of *Families* published by *Reader's Digest* carried an article entitled "Are We Teaching Our Kids to Drink?" The author, Stanley Englebrent, concluded that we are by example. He told of a hot summer evening when a commuter got off the train from the metropolitan area of a certain city and wearily shuffled over to the parking lot where his wife and two children were waiting for him.

As he dragged himself to the car his wife waved two martini glasses and a frosted pitcher at him. He saw the drinks and drew himself erect, a broad smile lighting his features. The weariness seemed to leave his lank frame, and his pace quickened. The commuters around him applauded and cheered as he drank the martini and settled down on the passenger's side of the car, the second martini in his hand.

Englebrent said the thing that impressed him the most about the incident was the wide-eyed kids in the back seat who were taking everything in. There was only one impression they could have got from their father's actions and the reaction of the other adults around him. Drinking must be great. People think it is, and their parents think it is. When they reach the age when kids often begin to drink alcoholic beverages, they will have no hesitation to drink because their parents do. Not only that—they have seen their parents drink under pressure. Therefore, when a tough problem faces them, the natural way of escape is going to be alcohol—the instant solution.

WHY DO THEY DRINK?

There are a number of reasons kids drink. They do so because of pressure, the availability of alcohol, and a natural curiosity that causes them to want to experience new things—to sample the unfamiliar. According to Jay Strack's book *Drugs and Drinking*, teenagers drink because of peer pressure, to escape the hard realities of life, emptiness, and boredom.

He goes on to say that the first mind-altering drug teenagers use is often alcohol. It is so easily available and is cheaper than any other drug. Startlingly enough, research shows that alcohol is being used by children as young as the fourth grade of school.

Clyde Narramore says that peer approval among youth is probably more important than parent or adult approval. They want to be liked by their fellows. Many will do almost anything in order to gain that approval.

I talked to my school age grandchildren about liquor and its availability.

"You can get it any time, if you want it," they told me.

"Do they try to get you to drink?"

"Oh, sure, but we just tell them to 'bug off.' "

Youngsters are looking for acceptance. They need the acceptance of their peers. If we don't give them a choice of something better, they're going to go for alcohol. Like their adult counterparts they ignore the fact that alcohol is addictive and can destroy their lives. They tell themselves that they can handle it and that addiction can't happen to them.

The Johnson Institute of Minneapolis, Minnesota, in their *Observer News* says, "A high proportion of kids who use alcohol or drugs are trying to alleviate depression, loneliness and anger." When you consider that 50 percent of all children will live in broken homes during their formative years it is easy to see why they suffer from depression, loneliness, and anger. And when parents split up the children often get the idea that it is their fault. "If they don't love one another," they say to themselves, "how can they love me?"

A friend of mine whose parents were divorced more than fifty years ago told of the turmoil and depression he went through. "Dad had to whip me every day to get me to go to school," he said. "You might say it colored my whole life. It still hurts to think about it."

Couple that sort of depression with the easy availability of alcohol, and you can readily see why many faced with such problems turn to drinking.

Liquor has been available to children in many ways through the years, but today, with their mothers at work, they often come home to empty houses where they are free to do as they please. They often have several hours at home alone without supervision.

I know of an eleven-year-old "latchkey" kid. He really didn't plan to get into trouble, but there was no one around except his buddies. The first thing they knew they had started drinking over at a friend's house. Fortunately for the eleven-year-old, he didn't like the effect alcohol had on him.

The boy knew his mother and dad loved him. They took him to Sunday school and church regularly, and his Sunday school teacher had talked with him about Christ.

"Remember," he had said, "you don't have to be lonely. Jesus is with you all the time."

The eleven-year-old had a choice. Many children don't

have a choice, and when temptation comes they are unable to resist. They feel accepted when they drink, and the alcohol allows them to escape the emptiness and loneliness and guilt they feel. With most youngsters liquor is no farther away than the bar in the family room or the refrigerator in the kitchen. The misuse of alcoholic beverages is epidemic in our middle schools, high schools, and colleges.

WHAT CAN WE DO?

What can we do for our young people who drink? Love them!

We have a tendency to look at the problems of teenage drinkers as different from those of adults. There are certain differences in the reasons they start drinking and the effect of alcohol on them. Earlier we mentioned that teenagers usually drink to get drunk, and the effect of alcohol on them is far greater because they are smaller and weigh less. Yet for the purposes of treatment, the methods outlined in this book are the same.

I was the director of the People's City Mission in Lincoln, Nebraska, during the hippie movement. A lot of youngsters flocked to Lincoln, the home of the University of Nebraska. When they got hungry and were hurting, they came to the mission.

Of course they didn't want to abide by any of the rules. They wanted to do things their own way. "I want to do my thing," they would tell me.

"I understand that you want to do your thing," I would tell them, "and I want to give you the chance to do your thing if that's what you want. There are no locks on the doors to keep you inside. You can swing right out if you like. But if you want something to eat and a roof over your head, you'll have to do things our way. We're not changing the rules to accomodate you, so you'll have to move on."

I was amazed at the number who accepted that because they were really hungry for authority. In spite of their protests that they wanted to do everything their own way, they seemed to long for someone to tell them what they had to do.

The daughter of a friend of ours told him a year or so ago that in spite of her protests and anger when she didn't get her own way during her teenage years, she was secretly thankful that he and her mother had set down rules she had to follow.

"I used to lay things on you when my friends wanted me to do things that I knew I shouldn't," she said. "I would tell them, 'My dad would kill me if I did that and he found out.'" Then she added, "I'm going to raise my kids the same way I was raised."

Another lad from Vancouver, British Columbia, was raised in a different sort of home. His mother, a single parent, was permissive. She never told him what time to come in, the kind of kids she wanted him to be with, or the sort of places he could go. Finally he got her in the living room and had her sit down.

"Mum," he said, "I've got to have your help! I want to be what I should be, but I can't do it alone! I need some ground rules. I have to have you tell me where I can go and who I can be with! I can't handle it the way things are!"

It is best if young people can be kept from drinking. But what do we do for those who do get started—for those who become alcoholics in their teens?

We pray for them. We share the gospel with them. We furnish them fellowship. We are long-suffering. We are firm in handling them and their problems, but we must never forget that a basic ingredient is love. They may be altogether unlovely when they are drinking, but we must love them—not for what they are but for what they can be. Love makes the other methods effective.

We may think that because a person is young he or she doesn't need the help of an alcoholic treatment center. That may be true in many cases. In others it may be absolutely necessary to get the teenage alcoholic out of the home and away from his friends. That is particularly true if the teenager doesn't respond to home treatment.

Some treatment centers have a special area to take care of youth. But that is not because the treatment is any different. It is because the recreation is different and because they are facing the special problems of growing up and the adults aren't. Those things need to be taken into consideration in working with alcoholic youth.

But, as with the adult alcoholic, it is most important never to give up. Treat your youth with love, and give him an opportunity to choose God's way above and beyond the way of the world.

FOURTEEN
GROUPS THAT TAKE ACTION

Many people are concerned about the problems caused by alcohol. What can be done about social drinking that is out of hand? How can we curb advertising that so subtly influences the young?

Current liquor ads often associate drinking with success. They have helped turn the nation's living rooms into cocktail lounges and basement recreation rooms into bars.

Some have suggested that prohibition is the answer and speculate about the possibility of getting a liquor law through Congress.

From a practical standpoint, it doesn't seem wise to spend valuable time and effort fighting an industry that makes billions of dollars every year and spends millions in advertising. There isn't a Christian or temperance organization anywhere that can raise the amount of money necessary to push a bill of stringent control through Congress and the required state legislatures.

HOW WE CAN HELP

So what can we do? We can pray. Prayer puts us in touch with a power greater than any in all the earth, a power that can dry up the liquor industry—not through legal action but through spiritual action. It offers power that can deliver men from the addiction of sin and bring them into the freedom of salvation. The only effective tool we have at our disposal—one that the liquor industry can never buy and can never destroy—is the power of united prayer.

A number of years ago I had the privilege of listening to a speech by Abraham Vereide, founder of International Christian Leadership, the organization that sponsors the presidential prayer breakfast, the governors' prayer breakfasts, the prayer breakfast in our Congress and Senate, and prayer breakfasts among businessmen all over the world. Mr. Vereide told of the way his work got started in Seattle, Washington. It was during a political crisis in which corrupt political forces threatened to take over the governing of the state.

"We began to pray," he said. "There were nineteen in the group, and only one was a Christian. But the others were interested in learning the answer to this tremendous political problem. As the men began to read the Word of God, they got straightened out personally. As that happened, they were able to be channels of prayer. They went about this quietly and even secretly."

In their prayer meetings, God seemed to lay on their hearts certain plans for action, such as getting people out to vote, precinct by precinct. Through them, God changed the course of that election and, as a result, changed the course of politics in the state of Washington.

From that beginning the prayer breakfasts were born. Since then, those breakfasts have affected the complexion of politics in many ways and helped change the lives of important men, many times allowing God to work through them to change the nature of politics.

The Bible tells us that we have an obligation to pray for men in authority (1 Timothy 2:1-4). If we have the same concern about alcohol and the liquor industry that those nineteen men in Seattle had for their state, and if we begin to meet in little groups to pray about this burden, we will see things happen. God may even deliver the nation from the clutches of the liquor industry and as a result deliver our families, our young people, and the alcoholics. He will begin to perform miracles as we get right with Him and become channels through which He can work.

We need to put the power of prayer to work in a concerted effort to reduce drunk driving. John Malden, a psychologist speaking for the National Highway Safety Administration, said this: "The drunk driving in this country has reached epidemic proportions. It is a national outrage that even when thousands of people are being killed or maimed each year by drunk drivers our society continues to accept drunk driving as a part of normal life."

In Gaithersberg, Maryland, Peter Weiger, a fourteen-year-old high school sophomore, was walking on a country road when a neighbor hit him and kept going. The driver of another car saw the accident and copied the license number of the half-ton truck involved in the accident. Peter was killed, and the driver was arrested. He was allowed to plead guilty to hit-and-run driving while impaired by alcohol and was fined $610.

In North Platte, Nebraska, a high school football star and honor student was killed when a drunk driver hit his car. The drunk was driving at a high speed on the wrong side of the road with his lights off, but the judge let him off with little more than a slap on the wrist.

In San Diego a twenty-year-old man who had lost his driver's license in a hit-and-run accident less than two years before, and was still on probation, hit a car carrying two university students, killing both. Though he had been involved in two other alcohol-related car accidents, was driving a borrowed car without a driver's license, and was traveling eighty miles an hour, he was given only one year in a minimum-security honor camp where he would only serve eight months.

The Presidential Commission on Drunk Driving brought in a scathing report on the problem and called for Congress and the states to "get tough." It called for the drinking age to be boosted to twenty-one, licenses to be suspended in cases where defendants are found guilty, issuing stiffer fines, sending more offenders to jail, and reeducating the American public to the fact that people should not drive if they have been drinking.

"Let's face it," the report said, "we're far beyond the 'drink sensibly' stage. Alcohol is a dangerous drug. It's not something that can be safely used sparingly—or in moderation. Abstinence can no longer be viewed as a puritanical concept. To many it's now a matter of survival."

We can pray for our law enforcement people, who are often frustrated by the ease with which drunken drivers are able to get their charges reduced and get back behind the wheel. The police need to know that there are people who are behind them and are working to change the laws and the court system that free so many frequent offenders. Several organizations begun in the last few years have been making progress in effecting such changes.

MADD

Mothers Against Drunk Driving has done an outstanding job in getting the laws in various states amended to stiffen the penalties for drunk driving and to make sure that drunk drivers are not allowed to go free on technicalities or because of apathy on the part of judges and prosecuting attorneys. In states where new laws have been enacted and vigorously enforced, the number of alcohol-caused driving accidents has been materially reduced.

MADD is a step in the right direction, but it is only a start—one small voice crying out against the injustices caused by a lenient, overworked legal system, weak laws, and the apathy of the general public.

Encouraged by the efforts of MADD and others who are deeply concerned about the need for stiffer penalties for the drunk driver, some states have passed laws fixing third party responsibility. Taverns may be held liable for the actions of a patron who, after getting drunk, may cause a car wreck. The courts in New Jersey have gone even further by holding the host of a party responsible for the auto accident of a guest who was attempting to drive home drunk. In Oregon a new law specifically holds a host liable for the actions of a drinking guest.

Efforts are also being made in Canada to get drunk drivers off the roads and streets. As a result, they too have seen a reduction in alcohol-related vehicle accidents, with a corresponding decrease in deaths and personal injuries.

Such laws are important steps in lowering the fatality rate of accidents caused by drinking drivers, but they are just beginning to be enacted. Pray that every state in the Union and every province in Canada will soon have similar statutes on their books.

We can get involved in the work of this organization by supporting it with our prayers, our presence, and our money, helping to enable it to spread its efforts to legislatures in other states.

We also need to pray that as drunk driving and other forms of excesses in alcohol use are brought to the attention of the public, people will be challenged to think seriously about their own drinking, and those who are addicted will seek deliverance. We should also pray that Christian counseling will be available for those who need it.

SMART

SMART is a new organization aimed at freeing commercial radio and television from wine and beer advertising. The group claims that such ads are aimed at the young and make drinking seem glamorous and a sure way to popularity.

The Presidential Commission on Drunk Driving has also called upon the communications media to help. The commission acknowledges the fact that ads for hard liquor are voluntarily banned from TV and are beginning to disappear from many newspapers. But beer and wine are just as intoxicating and dangerous. Specifically they ask that ads that tie alcohol to financial and social success be dropped.

We need to pray that these programs will have an effect of the future of alcohol advertising.

SADD

Students Against Drunk Driving is organized in high schools around the country. It works to get young people who are drinking off the streets and from behind the wheels of cars.

The group has devised a contract that they ask students and their parents to sign. It states that neither will drive if they have been drinking. The parent promises to come pick up the student if he has been drinking and to say nothing to embarrass him in front of his friends. The student promises to do the same thing for his parents.

Friends of ours with grandchildren in a certain high school where a group was being organized went to an informational meeting. They had heard that the group taught nothing about abstinence but was chiefly interested in keeping impaired drivers off the roads.

They were surprised to find that that was not the case. "We were very pleased with the thrust on abstinence," they told me. "The adult sponsors made it very plain that abstinence was by far the best for everyone, but if a girl or boy was in a situation where the driver of the car had been drinking, they should phone home."

"If you are drinking," one of the adults explained, "and you phone your folks to come after you, they will not embarrass you in front of your friends; but I would hope they would say plenty when you get home."

At the information meeting for both adults and students, films from the highway patrol were shown depicting some of the accidents they had seen in the past two or three years—accidents that showed all too clearly what can happen when alcohol and gasoline are mixed.

With the emphasis the organization places on the contract, it is quite possible that a group in a given school might stress only the fact that someone who is drinking should not drive. But the chapters we are acquainted with take the view that not drinking at all is best and present that clearly at the meetings.

Each of these groups needs our prayer and support.

Part 3

Ways the Alcoholic Can Help Himself

I am an alcoholic.

I know what it is like to burn with a desire to drink that is so overpowering that family, job, and friends mean nothing compared to the desire for alcohol. I know what it is like to wake up in a hotel room not knowing where I am or how I got there or what I did after going on that drunk.

I also know the joy of complete deliverance from the power of alcohol addiction and never cease to praise God for such deliverance.

The first two sections of this book have been written to help pastors, counselors, and the families of alcoholics to understand people like me—and you.

If you have a drinking problem, this section is directed especially to you.

I hope you have carefully read what has gone before. I hope you have studied the chapters on the alcoholic personality and the cycle. Whether you want to admit it or not, we alcoholics are addicted to ethyl alcohol. If you are going to break the hold alcohol has on you, you must face up to the problem and totally abstain from the use of alcohol for the rest of your life.

When I made the break, I had to have all the help I could get. You too are going to need help.

The purpose of this last section of the book is to help you in a very practical way in your struggle to sobriety. The counsel given in these five chapters has been given to hundreds of men and women in the more than thirty years that I have been working with alcoholics. The information has been gleaned from lectures I have given to those who have made a successful recovery—people from every walk of life. I have seen countless numbers who have successfully followed the road to recovery that is outlined in the next five chapters. I know that you too can successfully follow this road to recovery if your desire to be sober and respected in the community is strong enough to motivate you to turn your life completely over to God.

FIFTEEN
TRANSFER YOUR DEPENDENCY TO GOD

YOU CAN'T DO IT YOURSELF

"I don't understand myself at all, for I really want to do what is right, but I can't. I do what I don't want to—what I hate" (Romans 7:15, TLB).

No one understands the meaning of that verse better than an alcoholic. We want to do what is right. Oh, how we want to be restored to our families and to become respected members of the community! But our craving for alcohol is so powerful we cannot overcome it. You would have to search the world to find an individual who has more feelings of guilt and remorse, or feels any more sorry for himself, than alcoholics do. In the throes of our addiction, we are, of all men, most miserable.

And not without reason.

We realize, with vague uneasiness, that our personalities are breaking down. We know our ability to do our work is slipping from us. Our families are drifting away or are already gone, and our friends leave us.

We are caught up in a terrifying wheel within a wheel. We are trying to make a recovery and at the same time trying to satisfy our craving for alcohol. We experience one failure after another. Time and again we make a firm decision to leave liquor alone, followed by a terrible, losing battle and a miserable sickening drunk that goes into another and another and another. At last we reach the place where we are convinced that there is no hope for us, and we give ourselves over to the misery of existing from one bottle to another. We try to convince our family and friends that we are still in charge of our lives and can stop drinking any time we want to, but in reality we know that we are helpless.

We become strangers to our loved ones and even to ourselves. To get another bottle, we lie and cheat and steal with animal cunning in an effort to outsmart those who are trying to help us. We will make miserable exhibitions of ourselves before anyone who happens to be around, yet we are too proud to admit that we have a problem with alcohol. We hate what we are and long for help, yet are too self-centered to ask for it. Added to all these doubts and inner problems is a nagging thought that nobody loves us. In fact, we even begin to lose any love we have had for ourselves.

To an alcoholic who feels totally unlovable, the message that God loves him comes as good news. God's love is a mystery no one can completely understand, but I know its reality. I have experienced this love of God, which we read about in His Word: "But God demonstrates his own love for us in this: While we were still sinners, Christ died for us" (Romans 5:8, NIV).

How I Found God's Love

As an inmate in one of the Texas prisons in 1948 after a two-year drunk that landed me there, I hit bottom. I began to look for a way to straighten out my life and discovered Christ as the answer. I was led to this discovery when I read the title of a tract on the chaplain's reading table, *Why Not Try God?*

Why not try God? I asked myself. *You've tried everything else.* And I had.

When I first realized that I had a drinking problem, I took the geographical cure. I tried to run from liquor. Instead of succeeding, I wound up on skid row. Then I tried a tour in the army, thinking that would change me. The disciplined life would surely help me to conquer my craving for alcohol. It didn't help any more than trying to run from my problem did. I made a comeback of sorts after my discharge but soon began to slip again. That time I tried psychiatry. The doctor I went to attempted to help me understand my problem, but that was useless too. I even tried church, if you can call sitting in a service once a week "trying church." All I did with that effort was give false hope to my wife. I was still drinking as much as ever. As another alcoholic, you already know why none of those things worked. I wouldn't let them.

But that day I stood for several minutes staring at the leaflet in my hands. The title of that tract gnawed at me, even when I got back to my cell. For the first time since I was imprisoned I picked up the Gideon Bible that had been placed there five years before. As I read I made a startling discovery. God is holy! "There is none holy as the Lord: . . . neither is there any rock like our God" (1 Samuel 2:2).

From my days in Sunday school and what I read in the Bible I understood that sin cut one off from God. But now I made another startling discovery. I had a sinful nature. That is well described in Romans 7:18. "I know I am rotten through and through so far as my old sinful nature is concerned. No matter which way I turn I can't make myself do right. I want to but I can't" (TLB).

Up until that time, I had supposed that I was a sinner because of the wicked things I had done. Then I learned that because of my sinful nature I, Jerry Dunn, had drifted into alcohol addiction and had left my wife and family. I was a liar and a cheat.

I felt as the apostle Paul must have felt when he wrote, "So you see how it is: my new life tells me to do right, but the old nature that is still inside me loves to sin. Oh, what a terrible predicament I'm in! Who will free me from my slavery to this deadly lower nature?" (Romans 7:24-25, TLB).

God was holy! I was sinful! How could I ever be delivered from my sinful nature?

At Christmas time the same year, as I read the Christmas story I read this verse: "And she shall bring forth a son, and thou shalt call his name Jesus; for he shall save his people from their sins" (Matthew 1:21).

The thought fascinated me. If Jesus Christ came to be a Savior, I wanted to find out how He could save me. So I began to study the life of Christ. As I searched the Bible, I learned that Christ came to give life. "So whoever has God's Son has life; whoever does not have his Son, does not have life" (1 John 4:12, TLB). Jesus Christ said of Himself, "I am come that they might have life, and that they might have it more abundantly" (John 10:10).

I couldn't understand what the Bible said about being dead in trespasses and sin, but it wasn't very hard for me to look at my past and know that I hadn't been really living, that my entire life was a continual search for something I had been missing. Spiritually, I was dead.

Everywhere I looked in those days I saw dead men whose lives had been wasted away. I thought of my old drinking buddies. Most of them hadn't gone as deep into sin as I had, but they were just as dead as I was. They too were searching for satisfaction and direction for their lives.

I knew what I needed. My heart cried out for life, but I was so unfamiliar with the Scriptures that I didn't know there was a Bible verse that would have answered the cry of my heart: "I need a new life! Jesus, You said that You came to give a new life. You said that it would be an abundant life. That's what I need. That's what I want. That's what I take."

I didn't know anything about theology. I didn't really know anything about the death and resurrection of our Lord Jesus Christ, except what I had heard in Sunday school when I was a child. All I was really sure of was that I had a need, and deep down inside of me I knew that Jesus Christ was the answer to that need. I asked Him to fill my need and He did. It was as simple as that.

I was surprised to discover, when I began to consider what I had done, that I had entered into a transaction with

God. Somehow I knew that from that day forward I was never going to be the same as before.

God hadn't made any demands on me. He hadn't told me that I had to prove myself when I got out of the penitentiary. He didn't make helping me conditional. He didn't tell me that I had to start going to church and then He would hear me. He didn't even tell me to stop drinking. At that time I didn't have any idea whether I could ever stop drinking. He was there when I needed Him and came to Him in honesty, asking for a new life.

He will do the same for you.

The next few weeks were exciting as I discovered new and wonderful things in the Word of God. For example, I read in 2 Corinthians 5:17, "When someone becomes a Christian he becomes a brand new person inside. He is not the same any more. A new life has begun!" (TLB).

I didn't try to argue with what I read. I didn't try to figure it out. I didn't even try to understand how that could be. I had new life. I was a new creature. All things had become new. And somehow, at that very moment, I knew I was going to be delivered from addiction to alcohol. I knew it because of what God's Word said.

At that time I had to believe I had a new life. Now I can look back and see how new and wonderful it actually has been.

If you are doubting that such an experience can be yours, doubt no more. In all the years I have been working with alcoholics I have worked personally with men and women of all ages and positions in life. Some were rich and some were poor. I have dealt with people who were groveling in the worst and most disgusting of sins. I have dealt with chronic alcoholics who had almost forgotten what it was like to be sober. Yet I have never seen anyone who has honestly and sincerely confessed his sin and turned his life completely to God who hasn't been delivered from the power of alcohol.

Yes, God was for me. He is for you. God is for the alcoholic.

MAKE THE TRANSFER

In an essay entitled "Drugs That Shape Men's Minds," Aldous Huxley says, "We love ourselves to the point of idolatry. But we also dislike ourselves. . . . There is in all of us a desire, sometimes latent, sometimes conscious, and passionately expressed, to escape from the prison of our individuality."

Those of us who have been under the domination of alcohol know that only too well. From social drinking we have gone into addiction. We have reached the place where we depend on the bottle to escape from ourselves and the messes we have made of our lives. This is a vicious circle that all but destroys us. We must learn to transfer our dependency from the bottle to God.

That is the first way in which we, as alcoholics, can help ourselves.

We must recognize that we have depended upon alcohol and realize that that dependency must be broken, although we have no power to break it ourselves.

The first step in the twelve steps of AA puts it this way: "To admit that we are powerless over alcohol and that our lives have become unmanageable."

Alcoholics Victorious say it a little differently. "I realize that I cannot overcome the drink habit by myself. I believe that the power of Jesus Christ is available to help me. I believe that, through my acceptance of Him as my personal Saviour, I am a new man."

Our Lord Jesus Christ says, "Come unto me, all ye that labor and are heavy laden, and I will give you rest. Take my yoke upon you, and learn of me; for I am meek and lowly in heart: and ye shall find rest unto your souls. For my yoke is easy, and my burden is light" (Matthew 11:28-30).

There is just one thing that can keep us from transferring our dependency from the bottle to God—ourselves. We love ourselves better than anything or anyone else in the world. To acknowledge that we can no longer manage ourselves is difficult.

But once we look at our lives realistically and recognize that only God can give us the power through which we can be delivered, we are in a position to be helped. We must go to Him to receive that power. Then the transfer will be complete, and we will have rest for our souls as Christ said.

START A NEW LIFE

In addition to our reluctance to give up control of our lives, there is another reason we hesitate to come to Christ and receive a new life. We fear we won't be able to live as a Christian is expected to. We say, "I'd never be able to do all the things I should, so there's no use in trying."

We must remember that spiritual life starts with birth, just as physical life does. Christ said to Nicodemus, "Ye must be born again" (John 3:7).

A person will experience the new birth when he reaches the place where he is actually convicted of his sinful state and puts his trust in Christ to save him. Following birth, there should be growth. Growth depends on a knowledge of God's Word, which enables us to understand the things of the Lord and how He would have us live.

We would do well to consider carefully the principles of spiritual birth and growth. I have found a wonderful tool for measuring Christian growth written by Donna Smith, the wife of a recovered alcoholic, *The Recovery Handbook*. It will help you to measure your spiritual growth.

We must be very careful never to look at those who name Christ as Savior but don't live up to their profession. Such individuals either have never been born again or have never grown spiritually after they accepted Christ as their Savior. The failures of such people will not excuse anyone for not accepting Christ as Savior.

GROW THROUGH THE WORD

Every Christian must feed on the Word of God in order to grow in the Lord. That is especially true of those of us who are alcoholics. If we would continue to abstain from drinking, we must stay close to God. We must grow in the Lord.

Earlier I mentioned receiving a postcard that gave me the best advice I ever had. "Spend fifteen minutes in reading the Word and fifteen minutes in prayer every morning and you will grow in grace and the knowledge of the Lord."

That advice, given to me three months after I gave my heart to God, has become the cornerstone of my Christian life. I invariably give this same advice to the alcoholics with whom I come in contact. Those who read their Bibles and spend time daily with the Lord in prayer grow spiritually. Those who neglect it often fall away from what they have professed.

The Scriptures say, "Desire the sincere milk of the word" (1 Peter 2:2). A new Christian is like a baby who needs formula. A baby must be nurtured carefully through those important first months. No one expects him to walk and talk on the first day of his birth or even during his first few months of life. We expect him to crawl first and then to learn to walk.

Since the food of a newborn Christian is as important as the food needed by a newborn baby, we should consider carefully the diet needed by a new Christian.

When such an individual comes for help, I give him this formula: Read the gospel of John through very carefully and slowly, a chapter or two each day. Let God speak through the words.

"What you don't understand," I explain, "lay aside, and go on. When you have read it through once, go back and read it again and again until you have read it through five times. When you have finished the last reading take a red pencil and underline the word 'believe' whenever you come to it."

It will help to remember that the Greek word for "believe" means literally "to cleave to, to trust, to have faith in, to rely on."

When a new convert has finished the gospel of John, I

urge him to read the book of Romans the same way. "The last time you read it," I tell him, "look up all the cross references, a task that will take you into all parts of the Bible. You will begin to see the difference between the Old and the New Testaments and how one complements the other." This is a slow, painstaking process, but once the new Christian has finished it, he will be ready to follow a program of regular Bible study.

We urge such an individual to seek the help of his pastor or spiritual counselor in setting up a regular program of Bible study. As the new convert feeds on God's Word daily, he will be surprised at the joy he will experience in using the Bible instead of the bottle as the answer to his problems. He will find that as he grows spiritually he will come to depend on God more completely.

Here is something for the alcoholic to remember always. God loves him and wants to give him life—life eternal, which starts as soon as he receives Christ as his Savior.

SIXTEEN
TALK WITH GOD DAILY

Speak of prayer, and chances are that the hearer will get a mental picture of a fancy, polished, formal address to God or a few rhyming lines learned as a child. We tend to make prayer too difficult and complex, as though only those with a good education and a ready command of flowery language can pray. We forget that prayer is simply talking with God and that God listens when we call upon Him.

"The Lord is nigh unto all them that call upon him, to all that call upon him in truth. He will fulfill the desire of them that fear him: he also will hear their cry, and will save them" (Psalm 145:18-19).

If we have a personal relationship with God—if we know Him through belief of the truth of the gospel of Christ—we can know that we are never alone. At any time of the day or night we can call on Him, and He will hear us and answer our cry for help in trouble or temptation. Remember, temptation comes to everyone.

A friend of mine who is separated from his wife is trying to make a recovery. He longs to have her and his children back with him, but the road to recovery is rugged. On the day we were talking he had called his wife and invited her out for the evening. "Oh, I don't think I'd better go," she said coyly. "I've already turned down one phone call this evening."

A fit of jealousy seized him, and later he said to me, "Jerry, would you believe me if I told you I was tempted to go out and get a drink?"

Everybody has temptations. They come when we're not feeling our best or when we are irritated or disturbed about something. The temptation that comes to alcoholics is the burning desire to take another drink; to go back to the bottle and forget this rough road to recovery.

What does the Word of God have to say about temptation? "But remember this—the wrong desires that come into your life aren't anything new and different. Many others have faced exactly the same problems before you. And no temptation is irresistible. You can trust God to keep the temptation from becoming so strong that you can't stand up against it, for He has promised this and will do what He says. He will show you how to escape temptation's power so that you can bear up patiently against it" (1 Corinthians 10:13, TLB).

We don't know what methods God might use in making a way of escape from temptation for us, but we can be sure that one way of escape is for us to start talking to Him about the temptation. When Christ talked with His disciples in the Garden of Gethsemane, He said, "Watch and pray, that ye enter not into temptation: the spirit indeed is willing, but the flesh is weak" (Matthew 26:41).

We must settle it in our hearts that God is listening. All we have to do is cry out to Him, and He will deliver us. This was clearly illustrated to me after I became a Christian and was back home with my family and once more in the business world. I was out to dinner with some business acquaintances, and the other men had cocktails. The desire to drink was so great I broke out in a cold sweat. I cried in my heart, *Oh, God! Deliver me!*

Immediately a great peace came over me. My will was strengthened by the encouragement God gave me, and I didn't yield to temptation.

THE LORD'S PRAYER—AN OUTLINE FOR TALKING WITH GOD

Not long ago a man said to me, "I'm afraid to pray where anyone will hear me. I don't know how."

If you feel that way, don't be discouraged. The disciples didn't know how to pray either. They came to Jesus one day with this request, "Teach us to pray." In response, He gave them an outline for talking to God. (See Matthew 6:9-14.)

"After this manner therefore pray ye: *Our Father* which art in heaven."

We are first directed to call upon God as our Father. When we pray that way, we are calling attention to our personal relationship with Him. We are members of His family.

We alcoholics know what it means to be lonely, especially when we take the first few timid steps up the road to recovery. Any alcoholic has a tendency to feel as though he is the only one in the world. Yet he is never alone if God is his Father. God is always with His children, and they always have access to Him.

But that is not all. We who are God's children are all members of a large family and have brothers and sisters in Christ who are willing to stand with us and help to relieve our loneliness.

The beginning of a successful prayer life is the recognition of our relationship to God as our Father and unshaken confidence that this relationship is a reality. Paul writes in Romans, "The Spirit himself testifies with our spirit that we are God's children. Now if we are children, then we are heirs—heirs of God and co-heirs with Christ, if indeed we share in his sufferings in order that we may also share in his glory" (Romans 8:16-17, NIV).

It is wonderful to know that we can go right to the source, the very Creator of heaven and earth—and our Creator—and receive from Him because we are His children, and He is our Father.

"Hallowed be thy name." The word "hallowed"

means revered. When you revere a person you regard him with profound respect. When we pray, we go before almighty God not only with reverence, but also with praise and thanksgiving. We honor His holy and wonderful name.

All of us have days when we have heavy hearts because things aren't going as well for us as we'd like them to. When that happens, make this experiment. Start thanking God. Thank Him that you are alive and that He has made your body and, although you may have damaged it with alcohol, He has been healing and repairing your body and keeping you alive. Thank God for the beauty around you. Begin to praise Him and see what a difference it makes in your life.

Praise is the elevator that lifts us out of the pits of despair. When we talk with God, we need to come to Him with a thankful heart.

In the Al-Anon booklet *Wives and the Family Afterwards* the statement is made, "Avoid, then, the deliberate manufacture of misery. But if trouble comes, cheerfully capitalize on it as an opportunity for growth."

We must be able to pray something like this, "Lord, I thank You that You are my God. I don't understand this circumstance, but I know that You are in everything that happens to me, and I want to receive Your good from it. Praise Your blessed name."

"Thy kingdom come." Christ tells us that we are to pray for the kingdom of our Father to come. God is the One who keeps this universe in its proper order. Before Him every knee will bow, and every tongue will confess that Jesus Christ is Lord to the glory of God the Father. He is the final authority.

Man has rebelled against God and His authority. That is one of the difficulties of an alcoholic. He is a rebel. In his rebellion against his world, he wants to be king. If he can't be the king in the world he lives in, he'll create his own world out of a bottle.

On the road from social drinking to alcoholism, an alcoholic has developed a self-centered personality that says, "I love me, and I don't love you." He has a difficult time tolerating anyone or anything that doesn't knuckle under to his warped reasoning.

To a certain extent that is true of everyone, alcoholic or not.

But the prayer Christ gave says, "Thy kingdom come." When we pray that way, we are praying that He will take over the final authority in our lives. We want to make Him the King of everything that we think, say, or do.

"Thy will be done in earth, as it is in heaven." We alcoholics are a stiff-necked lot. It is hard for us to get to the place where we want to turn our wills over to someone else, even to God. And even after we have done it once, from time to time we revert to our former stubborn attitude of balking at God's will.

That is the reason we should daily renew the surrender of our wills to God's will. We should not walk out of our homes without having committed ourselves to our Lord and without having relinquished our wills to Him so that we might do His will all during that day.

Charles L. Allen makes this statement: "Obedience to His will today means that God assumes the responsibility for our tomorrow."

That is a challenge we alcoholics can accept.

Sometimes as we start on the comeback trail, we demand the solution of all our problems now. And we want to know what the solution to those problems is going to be before we give in to any plan or program. That may be what we want, but frankly, I have never known it to work out that way.

The man or woman who is still holding out because he wants to know exactly how everything is going to end before he begins is probably rebellious and still drinking. The person who says, "I'm giving myself over to You. Here's my will for today; make it into whatever You have for me," is the one whom God can help. For this individual

He smooths out the difficult places, unites families, restores businesses, and finds jobs. God has something to work with.

"Give us this day our daily bread." Christianity is practical. God is practical. He knows our needs and wants to supply them to us.

The apostle Paul, writing to the Christians at Thessalonica, said, "If any would not work, neither should he eat" (2 Thessalonians 3:10). He also said that the man who doesn't take care of his family is worse than an infidel (1 Timothy 5:8). God is love. He doesn't want to see our families go hungry. He will see to it that we have the work we need. "Wherefore, if God so clothe the grass of the field, . . . shall he not much more clothe you, 0 ye of little faith? . . . But seek ye first the kingdom of God, and his righteousness: and all these things shall be added unto you" (Matthew 6:30-33).

If we follow the outline Christ gave us in the Lord's Prayer, we will be following the teaching of this portion of Scripture too. We will seek the kingdom of God and His righteousness first and then look to our material needs.

That doesn't mean that we can sit in our office with our feet on the desk or lie in bed until noon and then expect God to supply our needs. It does mean that He is going to give us the perseverance we need in looking for a job. And if we really believe He cares for us as a father cares for his children, we will not become discouraged.

Let me illustrate: You have been honestly praying according to Christ's direction in your daily devotions. You have given your all to God and are looking to Him for guidance as the King of your life. You make the rounds of the employment agencies and run down the ads on this particular day, but there is nothing for you. In spite of that, you can say in all honesty and sincerity, "Thank You, Lord. I know that You didn't want me in any of those places. But I'm not going to give up or be downhearted. I'm going to keep looking because I know that You are going to open the right door. And that is where I want to work." Such an attitude will prevent frustration and much anguish and turmoil.

When we are in the place God has opened for us, we will have all that we need in a financial way. And if we do the job well, we will have the respect of our employer and those with whom we work. The problems we have had before because of our selfish, alcoholic personalities will no longer be evident because God has changed our lives.

If we do have problems, we can talk with Him about them when we talk with Him each morning. We can say, "God, I'm having trouble with this job You provided for me. I want You to work it out." And He will. I can vouch for that. It has happened to me.

I have my own quiet time with God in the morning before the rest of the household is awake. I get out my date book and go over all of my appointments with Him. I let God in on everything I plan to do. Then I commit myself to Him so He can give me the wisdom and strength I need.

When I was in the business world I talked over my business problems with God in the same way. It was a thrill to see how He helped us to run our business. Before I went into the ministry God seemed to make it clear that I should live by faith, trusting Him to supply our material needs.

We had some obligations because I was still making restitution for some of the things I had done in the past. My wife and I marveled at the way God took care of us. This experience was good preparation for our years in the Open Door Mission in Omaha and the People's City Mission in Lincoln, Nebraska. We could not plan on receiving a specified amount of money each month.

When we were in Omaha, Garland Thompson and his wife had four children, and Greta and I had two. There were many difficult periods financially, but we have seen God do some wonderful things. I shall never forget coming home one frigid February day to find my family huddled together in the kitchen. We had run out of fuel oil and had no money to buy more. My wife was trying to heat the kitchen with the gas oven.

"God didn't send us to Omaha to starve us or freeze us to death," we said. Knowing that we were in the center of His will and He would meet our needs, we asked God to fill that oil tank.

That afternoon I felt urged to go the place of business that had been doing our printing. As I visited with one of the men in the office, I wondered why I was there. We didn't talk about the mission, finances, or my empty oil tank. "Lord," I prayed silently, "please show me why I am here." After a time I excused myself to go back to the mission.

"Wait a minute, Jerry," the man said, "would you accept a gift?"

"The mission always accepts money," I answered.

"I'm not talking about the mission right now. Would you accept a personal gift?"

"Yes," I said, "if you want me to take it personally, I will."

He wrote out the check as we continued to talk about advertising and sales promotion. I didn't tell him until a long while later, but that check was for exactly the amount I needed to pay for filling our oil tank. Never again did we run out of heating fuel.

We believed that God would supply our daily needs. He has always done so, and we confidently trust Him to take care of our future needs. He will do the same for you if you make your needs known to Him and trust Him to supply them. He is always listening and wants to give us what we ask for.

"Forgive us our debts as we forgive our debtors." When you present such a petition, you are not bargaining with God. "Lord, I'll forgive Joe if You'll forgive me."

Christ taught that an unforgiving spirit is sin and blocks the blessing of God. One of the greatest hindrances to our full recovery as alcoholics is the lack of a right spirit toward some friend, associate, or member of our family.

I can illustrate this point by telling you about a very wealthy individual who had been hospitalized, psychoanalyzed, and treated with antabuse, the drug that builds a chemical fence around an alcoholic to keep him sober while he is trying to gain his footing on the road to recovery. We had dealt with this individual at the mission, but he always fell back into drinking.

"I really think he's going to make it this time," his psychiatrist told me.

"I wish I could agree with you, but I can't see him making progress. Ask him about his sister, and you'll see why."

This man had built up such resentment and anger against her that the very mention of her name set him into a rage. God could not deliver him from the clutches of alcohol addiction so long as he held such hatred in his heart. He is still undelivered and will be as long as his attitude toward his sister remains as it is.

If we ask God for something and don't see an answer, we should take inventory of ourselves to learn if some unconfessed sin is holding back God's answer. Once we do that and are confident that we are right with Him, it is good for us to remind ourselves that although God always answers prayer, He doesn't say when or how. He will answer our prayers in His own time, according to His will, and for His glory.

As it says on my plaque, "God will give His best to those who leave the choice to Him."

"Lead us not into temptation, but deliver us from evil." Christ is directing us in this petition to pray for victory over Satan so he will not be able to defeat us and destroy our witness and our testimony for God.

There are two great forces at work in the world today—the unlimited power of God and the limited power of Satan. Satan is out to do anything he can to overcome the unlimited power of God. He can't do this, yet he keeps trying. And because we don't understand, there are times when we are taken in by him and his cunning.

One of Satan's attacks is to tempt us to question the Word of God. He whispers to an alcoholic, "It isn't going to do you any good to pray for help in overcoming alcohol addiction. You're hooked. You can never get off the stuff."

If the devil sees that he can't draw us back into a life of drunkenness, he'll try something else. He may tempt us to take our minds off God by a selfish interest in material things. Deceived by him, we may unwittingly go into a life of fanaticism and thus become ineffective as God's servants.

Peter tells us that Satan goes about like a roaring lion looking for someone he can destroy. His attacks are varied, but all have a single purpose—to try to destroy our faith and to get us to turn our back on God.

Though Satan often succeeds in his attacks against Christians, we should remember that his power is limited. He can't do anything to us unless we permit it. We can allow him to get the advantage over us in two ways—first, by not being aware of his craftiness; and second, by deliberately yielding to his temptations.

Since we are creatures of choice, we can choose the right way or the wrong. The decision is up to us.

Satan is at work today, endeavoring in every way possible to get the advantage in our lives. If we associate with our old drinking friends and frequent places where beverage alcohol is sold, and if we neglect the Word of God, Satan will gain the advantage sooner or later and drag us down into alcoholism once more. That is the reason Christ urges us to pray daily that we will be delivered from temptation and protected from evil.

A verse in Revelation tells how a certain group of people overcame the limited power of Satan through their faith in the Lord Jesus Christ: "And they have overcome (conquered) him by means of the blood of the Lamb and by the utterance of their testimony, for they did not love and cling to life even when faced with death—holding their lives cheap until they had to die [for their witnessing]" (Revelation 12:11, Amp.).

Always remember this: Christ's death was victory over the devil. And we can be victorious through Christ Jesus our Lord. Because of His victory and our relationship to Him we can ask, with complete assurance, that God will deliver us from the temptations of the day.

"For thine is the kingdom, and the power, and the glory for ever, Amen." As we pray, after we have spoken of our relationship with God and have laid our entire lives and our needs before Him, we end with the acknowledgment that He is the King, and the power and the glory are to be His. The things we have talked over with God and have asked Him for are going to be done because of His merits, not because of us and our merits. The answers to our prayers will come about because Christ loved us so much that He gave Himself for us that we might have life, and that we might have it more abundantly.

"It is of the Lord's mercies that we are not consumed, because his compassions fail not," the prophet Jeremiah wrote. "They are new every morning: great is thy faithfulness. The Lord is my portion, saith my soul; therefore will I hope in him. The Lord is good unto them that wait for him, to the soul that seeketh him" (Lamentations 3:22-25).

SEVENTEEN
GIVE YOURSELF

Neil Gilkyson Stewart, in a May 1962 article in *Reader's Digest*, quotes a recovered alcoholic as saying, "Yes, there is a joy in sobriety—but probably not the kind of joy most people imagine. It's a joy of being able to cope with emotional problems. I used to be frightened to get on a bus by myself. Now I take on all kinds of things. There's no sudden pride in this. The recovery of the alcoholic is the work of years. It is a complete remaking."

Yes, there is much to remake.

In the throes of alcohol addiction, the alcoholic has developed a very self-centered, antisocial personality. If he is going to make a complete reversal of his life and no longer be addicted to alcohol, he must start learning to give rather than to continue taking.

Giving is not easy for anyone, for all are selfish and disposed to look out for themselves first. We alcoholics are more selfish than most because we've been so concerned about ourselves and satisfying our drive to drink for so long. It is going to be difficult for us to break the pattern.

GIVE YOURSELF TO GOD

We must recognize that we need help. We must want God to have complete control of our lives. Then we must come to Him, frankly admitting our selfishness and asking

God to help us. We must ask Him, by the power of His Spirit, to enable us to show the giving and sharing personality of the Lord Jesus Christ, who lives in each believer.

"Give, and it shall be given unto you; good measure, pressed down, and shaken together, and running over, shall men give into your bosom. For with the same measure that ye mete withal it shall be measured to you again" (Luke 6:38).

GIVE YOURSELF TO OTHERS—TO RECEIVE HELP

There are many who want to help alcoholics like you and me, but they can't do a thing unless we ask for help. Once we've straightened things out with God, we should go to our families, our friends, and the church and ask them to help us if we haven't done so already.

We may find that it's almost impossible for us to admit to a wife or a husband that we need help. We don't have to start with someone so close, however. Our pastor is waiting to hear us ask for his help. The chances are he knows all about our need and has been praying for us for months.

Alcoholics Anonymous or Alcoholics Victorious are both waiting to hear from us. Their organizations and programs are set up to furnish help for people just like us.

In addition, the National Council on Alcohol in many cities has local organizations that exist for the sole purpose of helping alcohol addicts.

Most state and local governments have programs for our help. Even a number of large corporations like Western Electric, Allis Chalmers, and Dupont have medical programs for the treatment of alcoholism. Employers everywhere are becoming increasingly aware of the problems of alcoholics and their need for help.

If we really want to get straightened out and back on the road of sobriety and respectability, we will find many people who are ready to help us.

GIVE YOURSELF TO OTHERS—TO FIND FELLOWSHIP

A couple of men who came up through the New Life Program and were on the Open Door Mission staff for a time said they didn't care for a certain church. "The people aren't friendly," they complained. "They act as though they don't want us around because we're from the mission."

A little checking revealed the truth. The two men came to church late—so late they were just in time to be seated before the service began. They would ask the usher to seat them as close to the door as possible. When the benediction was given they made a beeline for the door. Their haste would make you think someone was giving away hundred-dollar bills on the nearest street corner.

It was true that no one spoke to them. No one had a chance.

Fellowship is a two-way street. It must be given and received. The only way we are going to have fellowship with other Christians is to respond when it is offered to us. A church congregation has a Christian responsibility to be friendly and offer fellowship to those who come to worship. We have a responsibility to give them the chance to be friendly and to respond to their overtures.

All too often we alcoholics feel that we have attended all the services we need when we go to church on Sunday morning. We ought to be in Sunday school, the Sunday evening service, prayer meeting, and the men's or women's fellowship. In addition to the spiritual help we get from such meetings, we will be given an opportunity to get better acquainted with the members of the congregation and will have more opportunities for fellowship.

Let me tell you about LaVern and his wife, Verna. After his conversion and deliverance from alcohol addiction, they started going to a different church. People invited them to their homes after the services. He gave his testimony in the church, and a whole host of Christians, many of whom he and his wife didn't even know, began to pray for him.

"How can I fail," he asked humbly, "with prayer help and fellowship like that?"

When we begin to go to Sunday school as well as church with our family, the people there begin to realize that we are once more a family unit. They could see our interest in spiritual things and realize that we are truly changed—that we have new life.

To be sure, we may come in contact with people who will treat us scornfully for what we have been and not what we now are. I lost a very good friend when I gave up my pastorate to go into the ministry of rescuing alcoholics. To him there was one way to serve God, and only one way —from the pulpit. But such a loss won't be experienced often. Most Christians are excited about the fact that one who has been caught in the meshes of alcohol addiction has been freed by the Lord Jesus and is endeavoring to lead others into that same freedom. That is especially true if we make ourselves available to be used of God in the local church program.

I have never known of a person with such an attitude toward service who wasn't made welcome, regardless of church or denomination. Nor have I known one who, having given his testimony at a prayer meeting or a Sunday night service, was not greeted with warm fellowship by the people.

Then there was Lloyd. When he accepted Christ and was restored to his lovely young wife and two children, he moved back to his hometown, but not without misgivings. "I'll never be able to get a job here," he said, "let alone be accepted by the people who know what a scoundrel I've been."

It was difficult for him to get a job, and there were those who would have nothing to do with him; but he stood firm as a Christian through it all. And, longing to share his experience and the joy of his salvation, he gave his testimony at a Sunday night service.

There have been few meetings in that church like that one. The hearts of all were thrilled, and an entire congregation was solidly behind him and his wife and family. From that time on, he and his wife were surrounded by Christian fellowship and Christian friends. He had some problems before he got his life completely straightened out, but the people stayed by him, and he came through. Today, more than twenty years later, he is living a triumphant Christian life.

Not only are churches criticized for their failure to help alcoholics, but organizations like Alcoholics Anonymous and Alcoholics Victorious receive similar criticism. I have heard people say, "I've never been able to get any help from that outfit. All they do is brag about their past drunks. They haven't done me any good."

When people talk like that, we can be sure that they have never made a significant contribution to the meetings. They have never honestly become a part of the organization they criticize so freely.

In the New Life Program at the Open Door Mission in Omaha we saw this very clearly. In fact, the leaders of the group therapy classes could actually determine whether a given individual was going to make progress by his willingness to give of himself. We were quite certain he wouldn't be successful if he didn't share his needs and his progress on the road to recovery. When he left the program there would be a good chance that he would get into trouble with liquor and be back before long, wanting to be on the program again. His basic problem was that he was so self-centered he wouldn't share himself, and because of that he wouldn't receive the good things God wants to share with all of us.

Give Yourself to Others—to Provide Help

Helping someone else in need can be one of the greatest assets in our new life. If we can help another alcoholic to get the victory of Christ in his life and deliverance from alcohol addiction, we will find that we ourselves are that much stronger. We should witness whenever we have op-

portunity and take an active part in the visitation program
of our church. If our church doesn't have such a program,
we should encourage them to start one.

Such a program will be of great help in reaching the
alcoholics in our communities. Contrary to popular opin-
ion, most of the alcoholics are not on skid row but in our
neighborhoods. The only way we can find them is to go
from door to door, inviting people to church and telling of
the way God has changed our lives.

We can witness and help others through the AA program. We can help to organize an Alcoholics Victorious
work in our church. We can take part in the work of the
local rescue mission. We can tell the men on skid row
what God has done for us and encourage them to believe
He can do the same for them.

Sharing ourselves with others will do something for us
that nothing else can. It will help us to build an entirely
new set of friends and will eliminate from our social lives
those old drinking buddies who do not as yet want to be
delivered from their alcohol addiction.

When people offer us a drink from their bottle, we
should offer them a drink of the water of life—the gospel
message found in the Bible. We should talk to them about
God and what He has done for us. If we do, one of two
things will happen. We will win them to Christ, or they
will cut us out of their social affairs, which means we will
have more time for our new and loyal friends who appreciate our stand for the Lord.

GIVE YOUR MONEY

We have heard it said that the last thing to be convert-
ed about a person is his pocketbook. I've heard some say
that alcoholics are the most stingy people in the world. We
have never learned to give of ourselves, so we are quite nat-
urally not going to give of our money either.

Paul said of the Macedonian church, "And this they
did, not as we hoped, but first gave their own selves to the

Lord, and unto us by the will of God" (2 Corinthians 8:5).

In the next chapter Paul speaks on the subject of giving in greater detail: "But this I say, He which soweth sparingly shall reap also sparingly; and he which soweth bountifully shall reap also bountifully. Every man according as he purposeth in his heart, so let him give; not grudgingly, or of necessity: for God loveth a cheerful giver. And God is able to make all grace abound toward you: that ye, always having all sufficiency in all things, may abound to every good work" (2 Corinthians 9:6-8).

From years of personal experience with men and women struggling to gain sobriety I have found that uncommitted money in the pocket of an alcoholic is a dangerous thing. The first big test comes when the individual gets the first paycheck. It is at this point that many fail. They stop off at a bar, have one drink, and before they know it are off on another drunk.

Why?

It has been a long while since the alcoholic has had money that wasn't already spoken for. He feels good about it—proud of it. In his pride he grows careless again and begins to travel with a fast crowd. Before he realizes it, he has taken another drink—and that is it. He is soon "down the drain" again.

If we are truly concerned about making a successful rehabilitation, there are certain things we must do with our money. First, we must be cheerful givers. That does not apply only to the money we give the Lord but to all of the giving we do. God has made provision for us. We should be cheerful in managing our money in all areas of our lives.

Jonathan used to ride to work with me. He had conquered the problem of alcohol, but the first of every month he complained bitterly about the bills he had to pay. "I used to feel that way," I told him, "but I've changed my thinking about that now. I used to drink up every cent I could get my hands on, without thinking at all about paying my bills. Now I'm thankful that I have the money and the desire to pay them. Why don't you do as I do? I thank God and am cheerful about paying my bills. You'll find out that you'll have a lot more fun on the first of the month."

Next, we need to recognize that everything we have has come from God and that He is using us as a channel to perform His ministry here on earth. Therefore, we should commit ourselves and our money to God.

From the Old Testament we learn that people gave a tithe (10 percent) of their income to the maintenance of the Temple, the priests, and for the care of the poor and needy, plus freewill offerings. Some industrialists give as much as 90 percent of their income to the work of the Lord. Other people limit their giving to 10 percent. And of course, there are those who feel they do God a big favor by putting a dollar in the collection plate.

We used to try to teach the men on the New Life Program to give at least 10 percent of their income to God's work. The amount we give should be according to what God has given us. We should give freely and cheerfully because of our love for Him.

Once we have decided how much of our income to give to the Lord, giving will not be burdensome. We will look upon that portion of our money as spent already. The only decision left is to know where to place it.

We do need to be careful in deciding where the money can best be used. We have an obligation to our local church to help with the maintenance of the church buildings, the pastor's salary, and the various church activities. Perhaps we should next consider any radio or television ministries that have been especially helpful to us. There may be a rescue mission in our community. If so, they always need funds. And certainly we would want to have a part in some foreign mission program, helping to carry the good news of the gospel to those who have never heard before.

Since there are many worthy organizations who need our help, we should ask God to show us where to place our tithes and offerings.

We must establish priorities for using our money. If

we have given ourselves to God, we will make the first commitment of our money to Him. Next, we will consider the care of our families or our personal needs—clothes, food, and shelter. We must make sure that our household is well cared for.

Our next commitment will be for restitution. We will make arrangements to pay back the funds we have borrowed or stolen while we were on the downward road of alcoholism. Such restitution is most important, as it indicates whether or not we are in earnest about being right with God and making a recovery.

Should anything be left over as we make restitution and reduce our debt load, we should commit our funds to some sort of a savings program with a purpose. We must be careful to manage our lives and our finances differently from ever before.

It must be obvious, first to ourselves and then to those around us, that we are different—an entirely new person. This will encourage the fellowship and the cooperation from others that we so desperately need.

Remember this: When we learn to give of ourselves, our money, and our very lives, we will (according to God's Word) receive "good measure, pressed down, shaken together, and running over" (Luke 6:38). God wants to give good things to those who will give to others.

EIGHTEEN
LIVE A STEP AT A TIME

It took most of us years to sink into the oblivion of alcohol addiction, and we probably spent years as alcoholics. It might not take as long to come back as it did to go down, but the alcoholic must understand that rehabilitation is going to be slow and painful. The road to recovery can only be taken a step at a time.

Since alcoholism has defeated us in body, soul, and spirit and caused a complete breakdown in our lives, we are going to have to rebuild that which was broken down.

In order to build successful lives for now and for all eternity, we must acknowledge several things: (1) God knows the end from the beginning; (2) He will direct our paths if we ask Him to; and (3) we can only follow God's instructions one day at a time.

Almost nineteen hundred years ago Jesus taught the value of living a day at a time. He said to His disciples, "Take therefore no thought for the morrow; for the morrow shall take thought for the things of itself. Sufficient unto the day is the evil thereof" (Matthew 6:34).

A pastor friend of mine in counseling an alcoholic expressed the small-space-of-time concept in this way: "Just remember, life is a cinch by the inch, but it's hard by the yard."

Physical Considerations

One of the most startling things we alcoholics have to face when we begin to sober up and free ourselves from the anesthetic effect of alcoholic beverages is the realization that our bodies are actually weak. We begin to have aches and pains we didn't know we had before. We may be suffering from malnutrition or any of a host of ailments that could be abused or aggravated by the way we have abused our bodies. Our physical weakness can be most discouraging if we don't understand that it is the normal reaction.

We should have a complete physical examination to discover the exact condition of our bodies and to begin a health rebuilding program. (It would be well to see a dentist, too, and get our teeth in good condition. A severe toothache can provide a strong temptation to go back to drink.) Getting our bodies restored can provide another bulwark against yielding to the pull of alcohol. If we feel good physically, we are better equipped to throw off temptation.

Some of the strength we need to abstain can come from fully understanding our situation. We need to realize that we aren't going to feel good all the time. We are going to have normal periods in our emotional cycles as well as some high periods and low periods. The times when we feel unusually downhearted and discouraged or unusually good can be danger points as far as taking another drink is concerned.

When we are down we are apt to wallow in self-pity until we resort to alcohol. When we feel exceptionally good, we are apt to think we're big enough to control anything in the world and can take a social drink without stumbling over the edge of sobriety.

When we feel that the whole world is against us and everything is going wrong, we should realize we are going through a low period. Everyone experiences low periods now and then. Just knowing that can help us a great deal in our fight against the urge to go back to the bottle.

We shouldn't let those low periods influence us in our relationship with other people or our jobs. We shouldn't make important decisions or start big programs when we feel that way. Instead we should carry out only our normal daily routine.

This is a good time for us to see the other fellow's side of things in the right perspective. It is also very important that we spend extra time in prayer and rest.

If we recognize our low periods for what they are and realize that we are not going to be able to eliminate them, we will be able to go through them more successfully.

Those times when we feel exceptionally good can also cause us trouble. We need to have this thought deeply burned into our hearts—regardless of how we feel at any given moment, we can never take another drink. One drink will start building the fire that will send us back into oblivion.

When we are feeling our best, we can do our best selling, our best work. We should use those periods constructively.

Fatigue is another enemy of sobriety with which the alcoholic must deal. Once we have sobered up, we want to be successful. We want to make up to our family everything we have robbed them of during our drunkenness. As a result, we may work too many hours. We push ourselves beyond our physical limits in our struggle to get ahead.

Tension, overwork, and lack of proper rest can cause us to fall again. So can the failure to eat regularly.

Anyone who has worked with alcoholics knows that a good breakfast and lunch will go far toward helping the alcoholic keep down the demands of his body for another drink. To live successfully, a step at a time, the habits of the old days, when we thought we could take our food from a bottle, must be replaced with good eating habits.

Relaxing after we come home from work in the evening is another way to help our bodies fight the craving for alcohol. We should loosen our clothing and lie flat on our backs for half an hour or so. Whether we sleep doesn't matter. A shower, or just washing our hands and face, will be enough to wake us up and prepare us for the evening if we have to go out. And we feel so much better following such a routine than in the old days when we drank for strength to carry on.

The apostle Paul had this to say of himself, "I run the race then with determination. I am no shadowboxer; I really fight! I am my body's sternest master, for fear that when I have preached to others I should myself be disqualified" (1 Corinthians 9:26-27, Phillips).

FORMING NEW HABITS

Oswald Chambers wrote, "Beware of dividing man up into body, soul, and spirit. . . . Soul has no entity. It depends entirely upon the body. And yet there is a subtle, spiritual element in it. Soul is the rational description of my personal spirit in my body; the way I reason and think and work. Habits are formed in the soul, not in the spirit. And they are formed in the soul by means of the body."

We must remember that our virtues, as well as our vices, are made up of a series of habits. So if we're going to live a new life we must change the pattern of our habits.

So often people have the misconceived idea that once they have accepted Christ as their Savior, everything depends upon Him.

Such an attitude is seen in the alcoholic who goes down to the corner bar praying, "Lord, deliver me from temptation." He orders a drink and sits there, figuratively expecting God to send His angels to knock the drink out of his hand, pick him up, and set him out on the front sidewalk, thus delivering him from temptation. When he doesn't hear the flutter of angels' wings, he pours the drink down. Then he complains, "God didn't deliver me."

This attitude that the individual does not have to assume responsibility is taken by the alcoholic. God has to carry the entire load, and if He doesn't continually and dramatically take charge of every situation without any effort on the part of the alcoholic, the alcoholic thinks that God doesn't care about him anymore, and he goes back to the bottle.

This is just stupid alcoholic reasoning. We don't like to admit that we are Christians by choice and that God will never change that policy. He will continue to say, "Choose this new life. If you do, here is the way to live it." But our living is a matter of choice.

Oswald Chambers says, "We have to work out what God works in, and the way we work it out is by the mechanical process of habit."

So the choices we make as we think a thing through are the habits we will form that will either make or break us. Anything and everything is possible in the way of habits. We cannot form a habit without thinking about it, but once the path is laid, we can do a thing easily without thinking about it.

Spiritually, we have to learn to form habits by the strength God gives us. At the new birth we receive a new life that has the power to break all of the old habits. They can be completely dislodged by the expulsive power of a new affection. Most of us don't realize this, and we continue to obey habits we do not need to obey.

If we are going to bring our body under control of a new life, we are going to have to do it by new thinking. New habit patterns come from new thoughts. And those new thoughts are going to have to be godly thoughts, such as those described by the apostle Paul in Philippians 4:8-9. "Finally brethren, whatsoever things are true, whatsoever things are honest, whatsoever things are just, whatsoever things are pure, whatsoever things are lovely, whatsoever things are of good report; if there be any virtue, and if there be any praise, think on these things."

There is an orderly sequence of events in the shaping of our lives. As I think, I make choices. As I make choices, I form habits. As I form habits, I fix the direction of my life. So if I am to live differently, I must form new habits. If I am to form new habits, I must make new choices. If I am to make new choices, I must do new thinking.

Renewing The Mind

The power of a renewed mind is demonstrated clearly in the case of an individual who came to me for help a number of years ago. As a commando in World War II he had killed men in hand-to-hand combat. He had been captured, and someone had put a voodoo curse upon him. He thought the solution for his muddied life lay in alcohol, and by the time I came in contact with him he had become a confirmed alcoholic.

I was working with him and his family when he had a near mental collapse. I suggested that he go to the psychiatric ward of the Veterans' Hospital for treatment. In the few minutes we had together before they confined him to the ward, I told him, "God will straighten out your twisted life. Just claim Philippians 4:8 for your life. Think on good things, and God will renew your mind."

"Oh, no," he countered bitterly. "This is the end of the line for me. I'm not giving up without a battle, but I'll never get out of here."

"God loves you," I said. "He doesn't want you in a place like this. He's willing to make you new if you are willing to take His way." And when I left I saw that he had a New Testament with Philippians 4:8 plainly marked.

The doctors said it would be from six months to a year before they could even hope to see any change in him. Yet in six weeks he was released from the hospital and returned to society. He has been living a consistent Christian life since.

He simply took God at His Word. He read that verse of Scripture over and over again. Whenever the terrifying memories that had been destroying him came flooding into his mind, he would read that verse of Scripture over and keep reading it until those thoughts didn't bother him anymore. It wasn't long until the water of God's Word had washed his mind clean and renewed it.

When he went before the psychiatric board of the hospital, they wanted to know how he had accomplished this renewal of his entire thought process. He took the New Testament from his pocket and held it up, saying, "This is the way I did it."

We can do the same.

We must not keep thinking of the past, either of our successes or failures. We've got to think about the present, the good things that are around us now. On those good things we've got to build habits for a new life.

To fill our minds with good thoughts is not quite as simple as it sounds. We must deal with those things that cause us impure, evil thoughts. We quite likely will have to change our reading habits and be more selective in our TV viewing.

We are going to have to saturate our minds and hearts with the Word of God. We should be very careful to start each day by reading from the Bible and spending a certain amount of time in memorizing Scripture verses. Then when evil thoughts try to crowd in, we can counteract them with the Word.

We should also read other Christian literature—Christian magazines, biographies or autobiographies, or missionary books. We might want to join a Christian book club. If the family budget doesn't allow for the purchase of books, we can use the church library.

Don't be discouraged if you aren't able to rid yourself of all of your evil thoughts in a short weekend. If you persevere, you will break the habit of wrong thinking and form the habit of thinking on good things.

THE SPIRIT-CONTROLLED LIFE

The Holy Spirit is the master controller of the soul and the body of each person who has accepted Christ and has received new life through Him. We must beware that we do not try to separate the physical from the spiritual. Our new life must be lived twenty-four hours a day, seven days a week. The Spirit of God, if we allow Him to, will stimulate our thoughts, and our thoughts should stimulate our actions. We must recognize the close relationship between the physical and spiritual as we live out the new life within us.

"Do not get drunk on wine, which leads to debauchery. Instead, be filled with the Spirit" (Ephesians 5:18, NIV).

If there is any verse in the Scriptures that should be easy for an alcoholic to understand, it is this one. We alcoholics know what it is to have our whole lives controlled by alcohol. God's Word says that we are not to let alcohol control our lives, but we are to be controlled by the Spirit of God.

Just as we used to allow alcoholic beverages to control every area of our lives, making us liars and cheats in order to get another bottle, so now we are to let God, through His Spirit, control our lives. We should aim to please God and honor Him in all our thoughts and actions.

If an alcoholic has difficulty in understanding what it means to be controlled by the Spirit, he should think back to the time when he was still a social drinker and saw a fellow who was overcome by alcohol. He probably said, "I'll never be controlled by liquor the way he is."

Yet the time came when he was controlled by alcohol. How? By continuing to drink. Finally he came to the place where liquor controlled him, and he no longer controlled the liquor.

It is the same in being controlled by the Spirit of God. We don't understand how it can happen, but it can. All we have to do is to keep following the Spirit and yielding ourselves to God's way as revealed through His Word. Such a life is the more abundant life Christ promised His followers.

We never know what a day will bring, but there is an answer in God's Word for every situation.

As you study the Word of God and ask the Spirit of

God to teach you and lead you, you will receive direction in living a step at a time.

"May God himself, the God of peace, sanctify you through and through. May your whole spirit, soul and body be kept blameless at the coming of our Lord Jesus Christ" (1 Thessalonians 5:23, NIV).

NINETEEN
KEEP A PERPETUAL INVENTORY

One of the important steps I took on the road up from alcohol addiction was that of making an inventory of myself. At that time I knew nothing of Alcoholics Anonymous and their fourth step that says, "Make a searching and fearless inventory of yourself."

I had been quietly considering the new life that was mine and had been reviewing the past. I knew how many false starts I had made in my own strength over the preceding years. I didn't want that to happen again.

In my heart I knew I was different. I was trusting the Word of God. My attitudes toward life and the people around me were different from what they had been, but I had to be sure.

Assets and Liabilities

The thought came to me that in the business world we take an inventory and check sales and costs in order to determine whether we are making a profit or showing a loss. The practical thing, I decided, would be to take a personal inventory of myself.

I got out a sheet of paper and drew a line down the middle. On the top of one side I wrote "liabilities" and on the other "assets."

I began to list under liabilities all the things I knew

were wrong with me. Facing up to myself honestly was one of the hardest things I had ever done. I would sweat a little, argue with myself, and finally add one more fault to the liabilities column.

Everyone who deals with alcoholics knows that they are notorious liars. I wrote down in stark, bold characters that I was a liar. I am convinced that the moment I wrote that down I took the first step toward overcoming dishonesty in my life.

Once I had my faults listed honestly I began to write down my good qualities. That was more fun, but just as exacting.

When I had completed my inventory and had checked my list carefully, I wrote a prayer at the bottom: "God, help me to overcome my liabilities and to increase my assets. Thank You." And I signed my name.

From time to time in the early years of my Christian life I would take out that inventory and study it. Every now and then I had the joy of crossing out a liability or adding an asset. It was encouraging to have my spiritual inventory down on paper so I could actually see whether I was making progress. It showed me whether I was becoming more valuable to God, my family, and the community, or whether I was slipping back. My inventory was not just a one-time assessment, or something I did once a year. It became a perpetual inventory.

Not long ago I was talking with a fellow about taking an inventory. He thought it would be a good idea but felt that all he had to list was his liabilities. "I'm all bad," he said. "There's nothing good about me."

It is not hard to list our liabilities. If we will be very honest, we will see in ourselves self-pity, self-justification, self-importance, self-condemnation, dishonesty, impatience, hate, resentment, false pride, jealousy, envy, laziness, procrastination, insincerity, negative thought tendencies, vulgarity, immorality, trashy thinking, and criticism. That list may not be all-inclusive, but it is broad enough to stimulate one's thinking along the line of liabilities. We might be reluctant to list our assets, but there are a number of characteristics we should strive for if we want our Christian lives to be victorious: self-forgetfulness, humility, modesty, self-criticism, honesty, patience, love, forgiveness, simplicity, trust, generosity, promptness, straightforwardness, positive thought tendencies, spiritual outlook, clean thinking, and looking for good in others.

We must be careful how we use our inventory after we have made it. If we spend too much time considering our faults, we can get to the place where we can no longer face life because we are so disgusted with ourselves. That can drive us back to drink.

But it is important to judge ourselves according to the Word of God: "For if we would judge ourselves, we should not be judged. But when we are judged, we are chastened of the Lord, that we should not be condemned with the world" (1 Corinthians 11:31-32).

When we take a good look at ourselves and determine where we are failing, we can then make the needed changes in our lives and not have to be judged by God.

When we see sin in our lives, we should confess it—agree with God that that specific act or thought or word is sin. "If we confess our sins, he is faithful and just to forgive us our sins, and to cleanse us from all unrighteousness" (1 John 1:9).

And when we are forgiven and cleansed, we are once more in fellowship with God and able to receive the good things He wants to give us. We must keep in mind that if we are not willing to recognize the sin in our lives, God will have to chasten us because of it. He chastens those He loves in order to bring them to the place where they are willing to recognize their sin and confess it.

We have recently had contact with an individual who has some real problems. We have pointed them out to him, but he isn't willing to accept the fact that they are problems. As a result he is miserable and isn't able to receive and enjoy God's blessings. He is existing from day to day with God standing quietly by, putting pressure on him through circumstances to bring him to the place where he will recognize his sins, confess them, and allow God to deliver him from them.

Another man did the opposite. He was fed up with his old life. When he surrendered completely to God he went over his liabilities and his assets one by one, asking God to help him live the way a believer should. As a result, he was instantly victorious over his alcohol addiction. He was restored to his family. His testimony was radiant. God also gave him the joy of leading others to Christ. He is happier than he has ever been, whereas the other fellow is miserable.

In which pair of shoes will you be? The choice is yours.

We must understand clearly that God does not expect us to straighten out our lives in our own power. He knows the sort of clay we're made of. All we can do—all we have to do—is recognize our liabilities, confess them, and allow God to move in by His power and wash us clean. He will forgive us and liberate us from the chains of sin. But we must keep the channel open for His blessing to continue.

FACING TEMPTATIONS

I have found that my inventory has helped me to say no to temptations. When a particular temptation confronts me I say, "That's out of my old life. It's not a part of my new life. I'm not going to do that thing."

After I had accepted Christ as my Savior and had been released from prison, I gave my testimony in numerous places. The Gideons made arrangements that kept me busy every Sunday. I also used to give my testimony a number of times during the week. I got to thinking I was an important individual. One day, I was leading the early morning Tuesday prayer meeting when I turned to the camp president. "Now, look," I said, "these fellows are getting me so many places to speak that I don't have a chance to spend any time with my family. They aren't doing anything. I don't think it's fair."

He didn't say anything. He just saw to it that I was never asked to give my testimony again. That went on for six or eight weeks. I began to miss the activity. I began to check myself and realized that I didn't have the warmth and zeal for God that I used to have. My devotions in the morning had become dry and impersonal. I had to force myself to read the Bible and pray. As I checked up on myself, I saw that I was beginning to drift back into some of my old ways and was beginning to run with some of my old crowd.

My perpetual inventory sounded a warning that I had allowed pride to get the better of me. Consequently I was drawing cold toward God. "God, forgive me," I prayed. "I'll testify for you every time You give me an opportunity from now on. If You will just open the doors for me again I will not refuse another opportunity." That very day my drift downward stopped. God gave me many chances to witness, and I have kept steadily at witnessing ever since.

A perpetual inventory can help each of us to constantly measure where we stand with God. We should make an inventory of our lives and check it with regularity. Such an inventory will provide guidelines to lead us into a close walk with Him and help us to keep in tune with our heavenly Father who loves us and wants to bless us with all good things.

Keeping a perpetual inventory will do something else for us. It will help us to develop our personality in such a way that we will be pleasing to our fellowmen and will be acceptable in the fellowship of Christians. Not only will we have the advantage of good fellowship with our Christian friends, but we will also find doors opened for us to witness to others and show them how the power of God has changed our lives.

How can we alcoholics help ourselves? There are five ways.

1. Transfer our dependency to God.
2. Pray daily.

3. Give of ourselves.
4. Live a step at a time.
5. Keep a perpetual inventory.

Remember to keep looking up! The Lord will bless you just as much as you let Him.

SUMMARY

Dr. William C. Menninger of the famed Menninger Clinic wrote, "If any other disease (other than alcoholism) affected our citizens so much, a national emergency would be declared." All around us, in our neighborhoods, in government offices, in businesses, factories, and homes, people are suffering from alcoholism.

We have written this book so the millions of alcoholics and the families and friends they affect so very much might better understand the problem and might be better able to cope with their portion of this national emergency. It is our prayer that the alcoholic and those indirectly involved in the problem of alcoholism will be encouraged to know that *God Is for the Alcoholic.*

The late Dr. William Duncan Silkworth, medical chief of Towns Hospital and Knickerbocker Hospital in New York City, wrote, "It's very wrong to consider many of the personality traits observed in liquor addicts as peculiar to the alcoholic. Emotional and mental quirks are classified as symptoms of alcoholism merely because the alcoholics have them. Yet those same quirks can be found in non-alcoholics, too. Actually, they are symptoms of mankind."

I hope that you will see that the suggestions made for the treatment of the alcoholic are also good for everyone who is seeking his way in this confused, mixed-up world we live in. Yes, God is for the alcoholic, but God is for everyone who has a need to be delivered from himself into a new life. That includes us all.

SUGGESTED READING

Addington, Gordon L. *The Christian and Social Drinking*. Minneapolis: Free Church, 1984.

Costales, Claire, and Berry, Jo. *Alcoholism: The Way Back to Reality*. Glendale, Calif.: Gospel Light, Regal, 1980.

————. *Staying Dry*. Ventura, Calif.: Gospel Light, Regal, 1983.

Crabb, Lawrence J., Jr. *Effective Biblical Counseling*. Grand Rapids: Zondervan, 1977.

DeJong, Alexander C. *Help and Hope for the Alcoholic*. Wheaton, Ill.: Tyndale, 1982.

Dunn, Jerry G., and Palmer, Bernard. *What Will You Have to Drink?* Abbotsford, British Columbia: Horizon House, 1980.

Gehring, Robert W. *Rx for Addiction*. Grand Rapids: Zondervan, 1985.

Johnson Institute. *A Family Affair*. Minneapolis: Johnson Institute, 1979.

Johnson, Vernon E. *I'll Quit Tomorrow*. San Francisco: Harper & Row, 1980.

Keller, John E. *Alcohol: A Family Affair*. Santa Ynez, Calif.: Kroc Foundation, 1977.

Lutzer, Erwin W. *How to Say No to a Stubborn Habit*. Wheaton, Ill.: Scripture Press, Victor, 1983.

Mehl, Duane. *You and the Alcoholic in Your Home*. Minneapolis: Augsburg, 1979.

Royce, James E. *Alcohol Problems and Alcoholism*. New York: Macmillan, Free Press, 1981.

Smith, Donna J. *Recovery Handbook*. Lewiston, Idaho: Delivered Publications, 1985.

Strack, Jay. *Drugs and Drinking*. Nashville: Thomas Nelson, 1985.

Valles, Jorge. *Social Drinking and Alcoholism*. Dallas: TANE, 1967.

Williams, Roger J. *Alcoholism: The Nutritional Approach*. Austin, Tex.: U. of Texas, 1976.

————. *The Prevention of Alcoholism Through Nutrition*. New York: Bantam, 1981.

ORGANIZATIONS FOR ALCOHOLICS

Alcoholics Anonymous or Al-Anon. See your telephone directory or contact your pastor or medical doctor.

Alcoholics Victorious
International Office
c/o Chicago Christian Industrial League
123 South Green St.
Chicago, IL 60607

Alcoholics Victorious
International Service Office
1700 8th St.
Lewiston, ID 83501

America's Keswick
Keswick Grove
Whiting, NJ 08759

Christian Alcoholics Rehabilitation Association
Friends of Alcoholics
FOA Road
Pocohontas, MS 39072

International Union of Gospel Missions
P.O. Box 10780
Kansas City, MO 64118-0780

New Life Treatment Center
P.O. Box 38
Woodstock, MN 56186